POWER AND INTIMACY IN MEN'S DEVELOPMENT

Gordon M. Hart

University Press of America,® Inc.
Lanham · Boulder · New York · Toronto · Oxford

Copyright © 2006 by
University Press of America,® Inc.
4501 Forbes Boulevard
Suite 200
Lanham, Maryland 20706
UPA Acquisitions Department (301) 459-3366

PO Box 317
Oxford
OX2 9RU, UK

All rights reserved
Printed in the United States of America
British Library Cataloging in Publication Information Available

Library of Congress Control Number: 2006922138
ISBN-13: 978-0-7618-3449-6 (paperback : alk. paper)
ISBN-10: 0-7618-3449-4 (paperback : alk. paper)

∞™ The paper used in this publication meets the minimum
requirements of American National Standard for Information
Sciences—Permanence of Paper for Printed Library Materials,
ANSI Z39.48—1984

Dedication

I would like to dedicate this book to my wife, Kathleen Kropp Hart who has helped me to understand men and to understand myself. Her support and empathy are always present. I look forward to each day and the challenge that it brings knowing that Kathleen's humor and courage are with me.

Contents

Preface vii

Acknowledgments ix

Chapter 1
Power versus Intimacy: The Struggle Begins 1

Chapter 2
Depression and Rage 23

Chapter 3
The Exploration Phase of Early Adulthood 33

Chapter 4
The Transition to Thirty 49

Chapter 5
Marriage 71

Chapter 6
The Beginning of Middle Adulthood 85

Chapter 7
When Climbing the Ladder Becomes Too Tiring 101

Chapter 8
Changing Partners 111

Chapter 9
Later Mid-life: Consolidation or Change? 127

Chapter 10
As the World Changes 143

Chapter 11
Balancing Power and Intimacy 157

Chapter 12
Working with Men 165

References 179

Index 181

About the Author 187

Preface

This book is written from the perspective of a practicing psychologist who has worked with clients for over 30 years. I have attempted to show that the men with whom I've worked display patterns during their early and middle adulthood years that lead me to believe that power and intimacy are the concepts that guide their lives. I hope to show that men are not pathologically incommunicative or irrational. Yes, some are depressed and others are angry, but there are causes for their feelings and ways to cope with them.

In my role as university professor I've written books filled with the research done by others and me. For this book, I've reviewed the literature both professional and popular, but I wanted to write a book that was helpful to counselors, psychologists, psychiatrists and social workers among others and to be accessible to men and women everywhere. Men will read the examples and identify with them. Women will recognize the men in their lives – their husbands, brothers, fathers, and friends.

Another goal was to raise more questions than to provide answers about this complex topic. Reducing men's development in their early and mid-life years to two concepts is simplistic, but it provides a guide by which other concepts may be considered. Individual personality characteristics, race, socio-economic class, education, family dynamics both current and when growing up, and history of relationships are all significant and need to be considered to form a comprehensive picture.

A final goal was to make men feel less alone. Understanding that their feelings can be placed in a simple framework may be helpful to them. Further, I wanted to help men's families, friends and partners to feel hope for the men they care for and that change is possible.

I'm concerned about life stages that men face: moving from the home of their parents, work, social life, marriage, divorce, child-raising, career changes and more. Even though I talk about age periods, twenties, thirties, forties, and fifties and beyond, the ages are approximate. Stages can take place for men at various age periods. Age is only a rough guideline. The stages are important, but the age at which they occur is only an estimate.

At times I sound critical of men. Other times I sound sympathetic. I feel both of these emotions. Perhaps you will do the same. I hope that the tone is balanced.

Finally, I wish to reassure readers that I have changed the names of the men whom I've quoted here as well as identifying details. The examples could apply to many different men.

Acknowledgments

I respectfully acknowledge the many men who have been my clients and who have shown the courage to pursue the path toward understanding themselves. Throughout their pain they have shown confidence in me to guide them. I am touched and honored by their faith in me. I further acknowledge my friend and colleague, Dr. Don Nance, who has continually supported me in my professional and personal career and especially in producing this book. I also thank my friend of long standing, Ron Wormser, who always thinks the best of me and I of him. Finally, I acknowledge my two sons, Keith and Brian, who have turned out to be fine young men.

I would like to offer a special note of thanks for proofreading and editing to my teaching assistant, Tara Lally, a doctoral student in the Counseling Psychology Program at Temple University and also to Amy Winheld, a recent graduate of the master's program in counseling psychology at Temple.

Chapter One

Power versus Intimacy: The Struggle Begins

Introduction

"Men are only happy when they're in control."
"Men don't care about feelings."
    These charges are repeated in numerous books and magazines that describe today's man as an aggressive, self-centered robot who can't form an intimate relationship. However, most men don't fall into such an exaggerated category. Oversimplification doesn't help women understand men or help men understand themselves. Not all men want to control women because they fear or hate them.
    It's easy to see how simplistic generalizations can lead to misunderstanding about men's behavior. Everyone has a husband, boyfriend, ex-husband, ex-boyfriend, brother-in-law, boss or friend who either acts domineering and arrogant or behaves in a self-conscious and hesitant manner. It's unfair and counterproductive to stereotype men. Men may seem to fit the public image, but a closer look will reveal their hidden struggle.
The purposes of this book are:
    a. to provide information about men and their masculine development,
    b. to offer a model of what typically happens to men at various life stages, and
    c. to suggest some strategies for men to use in order to assess and change their behavior thus gaining the satisfac-

tion they seek and improving their relationships at home and at work.

The first purpose will be achieved by offering a description of the search for satisfaction of the needs for power and intimacy. Both needs form the umbrella under which, I believe, all other needs; for example, control, respect, money, sex, and love fall. I will also show how, in more extreme cases, men who don't attain a reasonable balance of meeting these two needs, suffer from either depression or rage or some amounts of both.

The second purpose of providing a model of male identity development will be gained by examining the chronological periods in early and middle adulthood. I will also show the dysfunctional responses of men to the demands of our society. Each period of life has typical challenges that men face. Meeting the challenge successfully isn't easy. I'll show how the search for power and intimacy plays out at each stage.

The third purpose of suggesting techniques for assessing and changing one's behavior will be attained by describing the strategies that I have used for thirty years as a psychologist working with men. I will provide case examples that illustrate the responses of men who feel threatened.

Foundation

All of the personality factors and resulting relationship dynamics describing men's development and behavior can be understood by understanding men's search for power and intimacy. Power and intimacy can be complementary. However, when men try to achieve power it's usually at the expense of achieving intimacy. Conversely, when they try to gain intimacy, it results in a loss of power, or so they believe. There's a conflict between achieving power and achieving intimacy that should be resolved.

Furthermore, I believe that both men and women need power and intimacy. Men and women find a deep sense of satisfaction and self-worth when they gain a sense of being capable and competent as measured against the standards set by society. I do not suggest that men or women give up the need for power, but rather to look at how they attain it and the consequences of that search.

Secondly, I have observed that men think, feel and behave as a result of how they learned to do so. I agree with scholars in the men's studies field such as Mahalik (1999) and Pleck (1981, 1995) who believe that men's behavior is determined by the messages they gain from various sources in their society. The sources of these messages to men about how to behave include family of origin, peers, significant adult role models and heroes, such as television characters, musical performers, sports stars, and other public figures. Problems result when men try to meet societal roles and perceive that they don't measure up or if they find the roles to be unsatisfying.

For example, when a man learns via movies or television to be a "tough guy" and is then called a "wimp" by his buddies, a problem arises. When a man hears the message to keep his thoughts and feelings to himself so he won't get hurt, but when doing so he then feels lonely, isolated, depressed and angry, a problem arises.

Thirty years of experience as a psychologist and observer of human behavior convinced me that most men are not afflicted with a pathological illness, such as alexithymia, requiring psychiatric treatment. Instead, most men feel overwhelmed and afraid of failing to attain society's idea of a man. Books in the popular press which form a rich description of men's development and struggles include *Iron John* (Bly, 1992), *Fire in the Belly* (Keen, 1991), *Why Men are the Way they Are* (Farrell, 1998), *The Hazards of Being Male* (Goldberg, 1976), *Manhood in America* (Kimmel, 1997), and *Man Enough* (Pittman, 1993).

Pete, a forty-year-old salesman, separated from his wife, had gotten the point when he told me: "I know at work I've been aggressive and demanding of others, like I am with Janet. I'm even more demanding of myself. It's been hard for me to learn here [in therapy] that I'm not as confident as I used to think that I was. Actually, I realize that I've been scared for a long time -- of failure. I remember when you said, 'I don't think you really feel as good as you say you do.' I know now that my aggressiveness was a way to convince myself that I felt confident about taking care of a family. My aggressiveness helped in my career, though. I never looked forward to a confrontation, but I sure fought hard when I got into one. What worked in my job has cost me a family."

As part of my work with couples and families, I've counseled men who've retreated from the demands for machismo as well as men who've tried to be more commanding and decisive. Both the avoidant man and the macho man are usually quite unhappy, and they would like to change. They usually don't know how.

One final point by way of laying a foundation is that changes, such as the much-discussed mid-life crisis, don't happen precisely at thirty, forty, or fifty or only once per decade on the decade. Men experience crises frequently, I believe, and unpredictably. Sometimes men act on the crisis and sometimes they do not. Specific behavior of men in crisis is described in detail by Diamond (1998), Levinson (1978) and Vaillant (1995).

Men's crises, although painful at the time, may yield positive outcomes. Many times, perhaps most of the time, it takes a crisis to produce a significant change. How the crisis is handled depends on a number of factors such as how a man handled earlier conflicts, the interpersonal skills he now possesses and his support system.

No matter how much they try to hide their feelings, eventually men will show the impact of the conflict. Sadness and anger are not feelings men will admit or talk about, but they will act these feelings out. Describing specific feelings such as happiness, sadness, or anger is rare, but displaying the feelings non-verbally or behaviorally is common, I believe.

Power

Men have a variety of social needs, but I believe that the two most important are the need for power and the need for intimacy. Only by understanding what men need and how they try to meet these needs can the confusion about what men "really want" be eliminated. In a time of confusion or frustration, women and men need only ask, "Is the conflict here between the need for power and the need for intimacy?" The answer is likely to be "yes."

People are motivated by wanting to feel good about themselves, in my opinion. One fundamental need on which many of their wants seem to be based is a need to feel competent or capable. Another fundamental need is to feel nurtured or loved. Having both worthwhile accomplishments and healthy relationships are common ways to satisfy these fundamental needs. To feel capable, a man often seeks to accomplish something or to control his environment. As many would agree, power is the capacity or ability to exert force or influence.

Some common measures of power are the wealth a man has accumulated or the influence he has over other people. The factory owner, the bank president, the builder, and the computer software designer may have gained power chiefly through the money they have earned and the things that they have bought with it. The town councilman, the minister, and the teacher may exercise power primarily through the force of their wisdom or expertise. Other people may respect and follow the advice given by these men's words or writings as they touch the hearts and minds in a way that changes people. Other measurements of power include attaining a social position or rank within an organizational hierarchy such as a corporation or the military services. In addition, social relationships can lead to power, as friends do favors for friends, because of the strength of the bond between them and the desire for a favor to be returned. Whether or not the source of the power is money, expertise, social/professional rank, or friendship, the goal is to gain power.

Levant & Pollack (1995) described seven features of the ideology that men learn. Their list included: avoid feminine behavior, hide displays of emotion, behave aggressively, rely on only yourself, achieve the symbols of power and status over relationships, be objective regarding sexual behavior, and finally fear and dislike homosexuals. I have seen many men who have learned and adopted these messages.

I believe that these messages influence men to seek power not only to feel good but also to avoid fear or anxiety. The messages of society heard most often by men I have seen in counseling demand that they:
- protect themselves from an unknown future
- provide for a family
- gain the respect of other men
- attract women

The man who seeks power to protect himself from future disasters hopes to avoid having to rely on others or of becoming totally helpless. He's often saying, "If I have enough money, then I'll be able to take care of myself if a catastrophe happens." If an unforeseen problem arises then he'll be able to solve it by being adequately prepared. Perhaps, as we become a global community, men believe that they have little actual power in a world of big governments, big corporations and big bombs, and this perception leads them to seize whatever power comes their way. Some men go one step further to say that they have only themselves to rely on in the event of an emergency. They're alone in the world with no one on whom to rely. Whether they're correct or not about this view is difficult to determine, but the result is that they carry a heavy burden and perhaps suffer additionally in carrying it without help.

The man who tries to obtain power so he can provide security, economic security that is, for a family is saying, "If I protect my wife and kids or my parents from harm and provide for them economically, then I will have done a good job as a husband and parent and as a son." The role of provider is a strong one in our society and heavily ingrained in our cultural tradition of what men are supposed to do.

The difficulty with meeting a societal standard is that it must be met continually. A client of mine, who's married, has two kids and is heavily in debt, told me that he thought that if he built a deck on his house he'd feel that he had provided for his family. Now that the deck is a year old, he's wondering if a remodeled basement would make him feel better.

The man who seeks power so he'll be respected wants to have others validate his opinion of himself. He's saying to himself, "If I'm recognized for my achievements by other men, then I'll know for sure that I'm a competent person." Unfortunately, in many work settings the "respect" often seems to be lip service and insincere acquiescence. Men often seem to have their commands obeyed and their opinions accepted without challenge, but they often mistake this reaction as respect rather than fear. Some men realize this distinction and others do not. One problem men face is determining if "respect" is genuine or not. Another problem is deciding if controlling the behavior of others is an acceptable substitute for respect.

The man who strives for power to attract women wants to control their affection and loyalty to him. Internally, he says, "If I can achieve power, then I'll be irresistible to a woman, and, she'll never leave me." Of course, this might be effective with some women, but several problems exist. First, if the attraction works initially, will it make the relationship last? If the relationship with this woman is based on her perception of power, what happens if she meets a man with more power? What if other factors in the relationship emerge for this woman that counteract or supersede the attraction of power, such as her need for intimacy?

Patrick, age twenty-seven, is single and works hard in the sales department of his company. He's on his way to gaining a powerful position and seems to want power for a number of reasons. He says, "I feel good when I make decisions and have other people carry them out. I like achieving the goals that I've set, and I continue to set goals for the future. I think that I was always competitive growing up, like in sports and with girls. I wanted to be known as a winner. I still do. I like being the salesman of the month. With women, I know that they're impressed if I dress well and spend money on them." It seems that Patrick likes to win. Success feels good to him, and he's never analyzed it further. He doesn't have to examine his life pattern as long as he continues to win. But what if he loses?

Seeking power to feel good or to avoid feeling anxious within the parameters that society has established is a clear path for most men. However, establishing a standard for behavior that is satisfying must be measured against the cost of time and energy it takes to achieve that standard. In addition, achieving the societal norms must be weighed against the loss of meeting other needs that are valuable for psychological health.

Intimacy

Intimacy is the degree of closeness people feel toward each other and is typically attained through openness and honesty, especially in the expression of their feelings toward each other. Both men and women share a fundamental need for being nurtured. We can meet this need when we gain intimacy with others. If achieving power is a way that men can convince themselves that they are capable and competent, then achieving intimacy is a way that men prove that they are truly loveable. When men feel loveable to people, they gain a sense of self-confidence and satisfaction similar to the one they get when they feel competent.

Intimacy serves an important psychological function, in my opinion. Only through intimacy can a person repair the emotional damage that often is suffered in the every-day world. A man can be nurtured back to mental health if and when he lowers his defenses and allows another person to help him figure out the meaning of the day's events or to reassure him of his self-worth. The opinions and reassurances of someone close to him are essential if he is to meet the challenges of life successfully.

In a healthy, intimate relationship, opinions and feelings can be discussed without fear of being judged. When men feel judged or evaluated by another, they pull back as this judgment feels like criticism of them. If they fear they'll be judged, and I believe most do, they'll avoid opportunities to be intimate.

Intimacy is gained only when a man is willing to lower the facade of the all-knowing, all-competent, emotionally-controlled and logical computer. To accomplish this task, he must feel confident that his partner will not take advantage of him in his seemingly defenseless state.

Typically, a man maintains power by protecting and defending himself against all possible forms of attack. In this way he is invulnerable. But if the armor he wears protects him from harm, it also prevents him from receiving a comforting touch. Furthermore, the armor of psychological defense mechanisms thickens over the years and becomes more difficult to shed. Eventually, the armor may grow so thick that coming close to another person might take years.

To further complicate the issue, many men equate sexual intimacy with emotional intimacy. Because they feel highly aroused during a sexual experience, they conclude they have experienced intimacy. They think that the physical act of revealing themselves is the same as the psychological act of revealing themselves.

It is possible for men to gain emotional intimacy through lovemaking, but quite often they concentrate only on the physical sensation and don't actually lower their psychological barriers to promote intimacy. Emotional intimacy is achieved by opening up to someone.

Some men are unable to experience emotional intimacy through sex because their need for power is so great. For these men, sex is another way of meeting the need for power. It's another accomplishment. They feel good having sex because they feel powerful, not nurtured or intimate. The more they need to feel powerful (because they feel powerless at work, for example), the more they want sex.

Where It All Begins

If men need both power and intimacy, are these needs equally strong? Are power and intimacy on the opposite sides of a coin so that if a man has a high need for power, he'll have a low need for intimacy? I believe that power and intimacy are on opposite sides of the coin, and because society teaches men to seek power over intimacy, most men do exactly that. However, this doesn't mean that their need for intimacy is any less than the need for power. Intimacy is ignored in favor of power. The consequences of not meeting this need for intimacy, I believe, are either depression or rage.

Most men spend their lives trying to carry out the messages that permeated their consciousness starting in early childhood. Because American society measures manhood by the amount of power one possesses, the primary message boys receive is to seek power over intimacy.

The forces influencing men to follow the socially-approved pathway are very strong. Parents, especially fathers, hold this view of how the world works and communicate this view to their sons. Sometimes, indirectly, by example, and at other times directly, through teaching, parents tell their sons what makes a man happy and satisfied. Most often, this message is about power, and in combination with the messages from peers and the mass media, serves to inspire a mighty hunger for power.

Martin, a twenty-five year old college graduate looking for a meaningful job in place of his current job as a bartender said to me, "Dad said that everyone is in competition with everyone else, and there are no timeouts in life. He made it seem pretty awful to be a man in the world today."

For many men the message has a rather primitive and physical manifestation about how to gain power. A client told me, "Looking back on it, I guess I *had* to play football in junior and senior high school. It was part of becoming a man. The whole school, teachers and students, plus the town were into it. My dad too. After high school, I wondered why I got the hell beat out of me week after week each Fall. I was a good athlete and played other sports, but playing football meant that I was a *man*. Playing baseball showed nothing. Playing football meant that a guy was macho. Now I understand it and realize how crazy it was. But when I was a teenager, I had to prove myself."

Parents acquaint their sons with their power expectations from an early age. In my clinical experience, I've seen that these expectations are inspired many times by:
- The specific unfulfilled fantasy of one or both parents (usually the father),
- The wish of one or both parents that the son have a better life,

- The belief that their son should adopt the parents' current lifestyle when he reaches adulthood.

The unfulfilled fantasy

In a neighborhood park, I observed a father tossing a baseball to his son. The boy was holding a bat that was too long and too heavy to swing comfortably while his father criticized every wrong move. The son heard: "Playing baseball well is important for boys (and men) to do." Implicit in the message was a threat: "You must do what I tell you to do in order to become a son who is acceptable to me." It's an unfair and eventually destructive message. Perhaps the father was trying to realize his own unfulfilled dream through his son.

The father who failed to achieve his own dream of athletic competence and wants his son to fulfill that fantasy is saying, "You must do what I was not able to do, so that I will be pleased with you." Having a son achieve a parental fantasy is a way for the parent, most frequently the father, to have a second chance of achieving his own fantasy, although vicariously. It's a way doomed to failure, because even if the son accomplishes the father's unfulfilled dream, the father knows that it was the son's achievement. The father then may resent the son for achieving a goal that the father could not achieve. Frequently, the son feels unfulfilled as well, because he accomplished something that was more for his father than for himself. The unfulfilled fantasy could be attending college or getting a white-collar job. The fantasy also could be marrying into a wealthy family or one whose social class is above the father's status. None of these fantasies are guaranteed to deliver the happiness that the father anticipates.

The father who achieved his athletic fantasy as a youth may communicate to his son: "You must pass the same test that I passed in order to be worthy of my respect and care." Some sons will accept the father's challenge and spend their life, or a large part of it, trying to live up to their father's expectation. Others will reject their father's gauntlet right from the start. They may rebel by failing in school, associating with the "wrong crowd," drinking, taking drugs, or impregnating a girlfriend. Sons who rebel may do so in adolescence, others in their thirties or forties. A rule that I have observed is that the more directly and forcefully a father pushes a son to fulfill his unfulfilled fantasies, the more a son will rebel.

A better life

It's quite common for parents to want their sons to live a better life than they have. One father told me that he told his sons, "I wanted them to have something more than I had. They're going to college, and I'm proud that I'm able to give them that. My father wanted me to go to college, but I didn't."

Another father wanted his son to become an engineer because engineers make lots of money, have social prestige, and enjoy some degree of autonomy. The father is a manager of a fast-food restaurant who believes that his life would have been more fulfilling if he had chosen a different career. He wants his son to have what he missed out on, and thus he believes, engineering is the route to happiness.

Parents who communicate "the better life" expectation differ in the tone of their message. Some express the hope that their children will achieve the widely accepted "American Dream." It's meant to be a positive encouragement to attain more of what a boundless country has to offer. Other parents, however, convey a bitter message that says, "Get for yourself what I failed to get." All of these parents put unhealthy pressure on their kids.

Keeping up the tradition

Many parents expect their sons to seek power in the same way they have. A father who is an electrician may expect his son to become a skilled craftsman like himself. Or a father may expect his son to enter the family business. The percentage of sons who adopt the same careers as their fathers is very high.

Kevin, a recent college graduate told me, "My dad went to college. My mom didn't. I don't remember my father ever saying that he wanted me to go to college or that he thought that it would be good for me to go. But I knew. It was always assumed that I would go. I never questioned it. I think the way he influenced me was to talk about the kind of work that I'd maybe like to do. All the jobs he'd suggest or mention required a college degree. I'm glad I went to college, that's for sure. But I don't know what I would have done if my father had pushed me toward college or demanded that I go to college. I was pretty stubborn and rebellious back then."

If parents communicate the "keep up the tradition" expectation through subtle suggestions and examples, the message will likely be heard. By so doing, parents show they are happy with their lives and believe that their lifestyle will be appropriate for their children. Generally, parents in this category experience the least rebellion by their children, and the children experience the least disappointment. For more on this topic read: *Finding Our Fathers*: *The Unfinished Business of Manhood* (Osherson, 1986).

Living with Anxiety

The way a man reacts to major life events such as career entry, marriage, death, and birth is influenced not only by the expectations he's adopted from his parents but also by the anxiety produced by these events. The anxiety a man experiences at any stage of life is related to how much anxiety he experienced earlier and how he learned to cope with it.

There are men who fear the challenges that confront them and seek the safest avenue. These men look for high security jobs and avoid confrontation in their personal and professional lives. They avoid marriage or long-term relationships and children or else seek wives, friends, and neighbors who ask little of them or about them. They avoid seeking power because they're anxious about failing. Some are anxious that if they do succeed, they'll have to continue to the risk again and again.

Other men feel confident about their abilities to handle the responsibilities and risks and boldly plunge into the world. They'll look for intellectual challenges in their jobs and accept conflict in their professional and personal relationships. They care for others and ask to be cared for in return. They accept the possibility of failure as a natural consequence of taking risks.

There are, of course, all sorts of variations. Some men experience little strain in adolescence but have a tough time at age thirty or forty. Men who enjoy the confidence that comes from early success may later stumble and lose faith in themselves. Evidently, they haven't gained the strength to withstand the shocks, bruises, and disappointments that the real world hands out. By not having coped with anxiety earlier, they haven't developed the skills to manage anxiety-producing events later. Early pain often provides a learning experience so that they can better cope with pain later, and possibly reduce or avoid pain altogether.

A man at eighteen leaving home for work, college, or the service, or a man at twenty-two ending college, his tour in the service, or a dead-end job, encounters a fair amount of anxiety. To some extent, how well he will cope with these current transitions depends on how well he learned to cope with earlier trials.

Here is the experience of Martin, one of my clients (the twenty-five year old college graduate and bartender looking for a better job): "Every growing-up point in my adolescence was a trauma. I didn't get my driver's license when my friends did. To some extent, my parents offered little encouragement, like teaching me or getting me driving lessons. They always seemed to be too busy and thought that it wasn't important. It was important to me! And I started dating late. Again, my parents ignored my interest in girls and made my interests seem odd or inappropriate or something. When I wanted to get a part-time job, my parents gave me a major hassle. They saw no reason why I should work when I already had enough money from the allowance they gave me. I had little argument to offer, other than the other kids are doing it. A pretty lame argument, I admit. It just seemed that my wishes were abnormal or unreasonable."

As a result he said, "I always tried to figure out which choice would get the least negative results. Do you see what I mean? I tried to pick the safest path instead of the one that may really have been the right one for me. I'm still anxious about making decisions and going out in the world. I never got confident, although I've been successful in the part-time jobs I've had and in getting through college." Clearly, Martin had experienced anxiety at transition points but learned few skills that would help him in the future. Perhaps his parents were only conveying their anxiety about the world to Martin, but he believed that they were expressing their doubts about him.

In contrast, Kevin (also twenty-five and a college graduate, working as a copy editor for a magazine) recalled, "My parents supported me when I wanted to get a part-time job, and I'm glad they did. They told me I could do it, but when I wanted to. Sure, I was anxious about getting my license, dating, and working, but I wanted to try. My part-time job during high school at the meat market taught me how to cut meat, say Italian curses, tolerate demanding customers, bet on football pools, and see how adults, other than my parents, live their lives. I felt successful." Kevin's perception of himself is that despite the anxiety he experienced, he was successful. He learned valuable coping skills. These skills in addition to confidence characterize Kevin's ability to cope with transition points in the future.

Three Common Life Themes

One life theme for many men is to seek power and avoid intimacy. Many men associate intimacy with weakness and vulnerability. Not a friend, a sibling, a spouse, or a coworker can know what they think or feel, because the mask of emotional calm must be worn at all times. Men hear and believe the message: "A real man never shows weakness and vulnerability by displaying sadness, tenderness or loneliness, and never lets anyone get close enough to harm him."

To seek intimacy means to become vulnerable, emotionally expressive, reflective, and open. All of which make men feel less powerful, according to what they have learned from all the sources around them.

Men pay a high price for hiding their emotions behind a facade. They are unable to forge and enjoy friendships with people at work, family or friends, or even a wife. Such emotional withdrawal is unhealthy. In time, it produces stress, illness, job inefficiency, poor parenting, and marital conflict. Opening up is the most frightening thing a man can do because to do so might allow others to take advantage of him.

Jim is a thirty-two year old man who sought power for a long time, only to find his world come crashing down. He's married with three children, but spent little time with them until his wife started to fall apart psychologically and needing treatment for anxiety and depression. He used to spend about sixty-five hours a week at work in his job as manager in a large company.

"I hate to admit it, but I've spent a lot of time trying to feel powerful. Somehow it's more acceptable to me to say that I want to be rich than to be powerful, but it's the same thing. In my case I tried to be important in my career and respected by others rather than rich."

"I guess I followed my dad's footsteps. He was a hard-working guy. He valued other people's opinions of him. I remember once he told me that the mayor had called him on the phone to ask if he could recommend someone for a city job that was open. I heard that story a dozen times. And the one about his high school baseball team going to the state championship, and his Army buddies and the important jobs they have now. One's a lawyer, one's a big farmer, and one's a coach somewhere. Between my Dad and my teachers and the other people I respected, it's easy to see how I got the message that I had to push hard against other people in order to succeed. And to succeed meant to be important."

"I really bought the American dream that in order to be okay I had to be striving all of the time. And if I were striving all the time then I would be successful eventually. But even if I weren't successful, I'd still be a man in the eyes of my friends and family, and society in general. I tried to be a man even though it was killing me. I worked so hard to be tough, calculating, shrewd and in charge that I lost all feeling of sensitivity and concern for others. I just never had the time. No, I never took the time to feel anything. I'd still be the same person except that I got so exhausted, felt lousy; kind of bitter and lonely. My family started to fall apart. Now I've reassessed my life, and I'm making some changes. Intimacy? Well, I've gotten a lot better at being close to others now that I'm not in a race with them to be such a big shot."

A second and frequent theme for many men is to adopt a Jekyll-and-Hyde lifestyle, seeking power at work and intimacy at home. They separate work and home completely. I mean no work at home, no business phone calls, no discussion of the workday, and no social relationships with co-workers.

The problem with such an approach is that it takes lots of energy to make the change from meeting power needs to meeting intimacy needs. It's like taking off a suit of armor at the end of each day and putting it on again each morning. Most men do this to some degree, but a major switch every day wears a man down. It can be seen most clearly when men go on vacation. It takes two or three days for them to relax. "I used to feel anxious and restless for a day or so", one man told me, describing his typical vacation wind-down. "Then I felt depressed for a day or two. Finally, I felt okay."

A third and less frequent life theme that I've seen is for men to deny that they want the symbols of power at all and seek to meet their needs for intimacy. By denying that they have any needs for power they avoid the search for power, perhaps by having a wife who will seek it for them. Some of these men seek intimacy through marriage and children. These men may find a satisfying niche in life, except that they may be plagued by the knowledge that they didn't really achieve what "real men" are supposed to achieve.

By finding and keeping a job with no chance of advancement or challenge and little chance of failure, these men seem relieved of the fear of competing and failing. But often, to preserve their self-esteem, these men delude themselves with rationalizations such as: "I could have been powerful, but I wanted other things instead, like freedom from the rat race, from being bossed around by others, and having to conform." The motto of these men is: "It's better not to try than to try and then to fail."

Avoiding the grab for power is reasonable if a man can accept that his choice for a lifestyle is very different from that of so many of his peers and that he's just as much a man as anyone else.

It's tough to admit that the rat race is a killer and then to seek intimacy without feeling that this choice was second-best.

Men who achieve a balance of power and intimacy eventually wonder why they didn't do so decades earlier. Typically, the reason is that they couldn't see the world in a way that allowed them to live their lives any differently. Now they live a life that is quite different; that is, indeed, almost a new life because their relationships with others are so different. Can men learn to give up the mad scramble for power in favor of a more balanced life that includes both power and intimacy without needing a crisis to prompt them?

Integrating Power and Intimacy

Power and intimacy are not at opposite ends of the same scale. Men are taught in our society to value power over intimacy and see many examples of how to gain power. Men have the same need for power as they do for intimacy. What they recognize or seek varies widely. A few seek intimacy over power. Some men search for both power and intimacy. Others look for neither power nor intimacy, but such men are rare in my clinical experience. The point is that men can and should, for optimal mental health, have both power and intimacy. Each complements the other.

Therefore, the man who seeks power does not have to give up that quest in order to obtain intimacy. Nor does the man who wants intimacy have to abandon his need for power. The key issue is meeting both needs.

Don is a thirty-five year old man who feels comfortable with the intimacy in his life. Don works as an engineer, lives in the suburbs of a major city near where he grew up and went to college. Don is married to a woman also from the area, has two kids ages 8 and 5 and is in frequent contact with his parents and siblings. He describes his feelings and contacts with family and friends as both warm and important. He's learned to achieve both power and intimacy. Don states, "I knew that achievement was the thing for men to do, but I never wanted it to be at the expense of someone else's happiness, especially my family's. I wanted to have an impact on others, and my personality was the thing that seemed to do it. So I try to be a good friend, mostly by being a good listener. It's amazing what a little attention and listening will do."

"Growing up was fine, although we didn't have much money. My family all pulled together and was supportive of each other. They always talked about what was happening, at school, with friends, and everything."

"As an adult, I enjoy women more than men because women are more open. Some of my men friends are aggressive. Others are more passive. They're all pretty open to me, and I can open up to them. Men who play the competitive game just disappoint me. We can't talk about things that are important."

"A woman once told me that I always seemed "rested" no matter what time of the day or night she saw me. I think that I just don't burn myself out by getting into the race for success like other men, or else I gain success by working with others rather than against them." Although Don may not know exactly how he did it, he's done a fine job of adding intimacy to his life, and his life shows the effect. Some of his success, maybe a lot of it, is based on his being raised in an open, supportive, and loving family.

Unfortunately, many men seek to satisfy their need for power in ways that prevent them from expressing and satisfying their needs for intimacy. The reverse is also true; that is, many men attempt to satisfy high needs for intimacy in ways that keep them from achieving power.

A typical problematic behavior occurs when a man seeking maximum power builds a shell of invulnerability around him, rendering him incapable of experiencing and expressing feelings. This makes intimacy all but impossible. Conversely, a man seeking a high degree of intimacy will abandon the assertive and controlled behavior that is necessary to achieve power. Power is historically achieved in America by conquering obstacles with intellectual and physical skills, while lowering barriers and expressing feelings gain intimacy. Other methods, as explained later, exist and are highly likely to be successful.

Another problem exists in the man who is most unhappy with himself who has not learned when and in what situations to seek power nor when and in what situations to seek intimacy. At certain moments it may be more appropriate for him to seek more power and less intimacy, and vice versa, depending on the circumstances of his life. For example, sometimes it may be advantageous to seize the business opportunities that lie ahead thus pushing aside intimacy needs. At other times it's best to satisfy intimacy needs and let the chance for power pass by. The trick is to know when to respond to the need for power and when to respond to the need for intimacy. How men master this trick is described in subsequent chapters.

Consider the case of Dan, age twenty-nine and a bright attorney, lost in a large firm where everyone wants to get to the top. He worked twelve to sixteen hours a day and took work home on weekends. His boss seemed to be pleased with his diligence although not necessarily with his brilliance. He seemed to work harder than necessary but rarely took the initiative. When his live-in girlfriend left him, he became depressed and sought counseling with me. With a lot of effort, he began to realize that his climb up the ladder was self-destructive and without a guarantee of success.

First, he talked with a senior partner about his career path and received career advice. This senior partner became Dan's mentor.

Next, Dan stopped working so many hours a day and no longer took work home with him. He delegated work and took on fewer new projects. He listened to his colleagues and his superiors and responded to them instead of doing their bidding blindly. Dan's secretary told him how much she liked his new self-confidence and how much more successful he'd been lately (even though no new successes actually had been achieved). He realized that the way he had attempted to gain power had been only minimally successful, and he felt lonely, empty, and detached. As a result he began saying "no" to increased responsibility and work, thus freeing himself to seek intimate relationships with others and gain their respect for his intelligent and honest opinions. When he found out that people - partners and clients alike – didn't want a machine, his job got a lot easier.

Scott, a twenty-nine year old salesman with two small children had been separated from his wife for three months. He had been in almost constant conflict with his boss prior to the separation becoming common knowledge. While in therapy, Scott changed the direction of his life and was aided by a significant encounter with his boss. The boss, a gruff, demanding man, one day gently confided that he wished he'd spent more time with his kids when they were young. Apparently, the boss had seen that this young power-seeking employee was headed on a course much like his own; a course that would produce power but few relationships that would bring him comfort. The boss was giving advice that he wished someone had given him many years before.

Then there is Larry, age twenty-eight, a successful hospital administrator who is married, with one child. His high blood pressure sent him into a stress-education program. He integrated power and intimacy only after a shock. "I was on a vacation with my family and I had trouble relaxing for the first few days that we were at the cottage. I kept on trying to be an administrator with my family. It was just making my blood pressure go higher not lower. Eventually I settled down, and then I realized what I was doing to myself and to my wife and children. I decided on that vacation that I wanted to feel like I did on vacation all the time. I stopped trying to prove myself to others and to myself. I accepted that I'd never be rich or at the top of my field, and that was fine as long as I could feel like a human being and not a machine." Time will tell if Larry can adopt new ways of achieving power that will be less destructive to his intimate relationships.

Achieving Intimacy and Power

How can men achieve power and intimacy needs simultaneously? That's a tough question and one with different answers for different men. Recognizing one's need for intimacy is the first step.

Unfortunately, most men, in my experience, wait until the level of their stress rises to a critical level and then they make a large and sudden change, such as quitting their job, leaving their wives, or moving to a new area. During such a radical transition, these men might make some very bad decisions and still not become aware of their need for intimacy.

Some men discover their need for intimacy by suffering a life-threatening accident or heart attack, losing their job or a loved one. For others, it's the disappointment and frustration accumulated over a decade or two that prompts them to slowly begin the path toward intimacy. Unfortunately, most men fail to recognize the initial symptoms of a lack of intimacy. They react only after the pain becomes intense and unbearable.

Some men are different. Early on, they realize the importance of establishing a balance between power and intimacy, and they work hard at specific ways to maintain it.

Jeff is a twenty-four year old married man with a new baby. He's a bookkeeper for a small automobile dealer. He made intimacy a part of his life starting at early adulthood. "I believed the divorce statistics and that it could happen to me if I wasn't careful. I set up rules about what I'd do and wouldn't do about my career. I wouldn't move no matter what. I wouldn't travel. Wouldn't take work home. And I'd do my best to be home for dinner. Sometimes I'd work at home on the weekends to catch up, but I never went into the office on the weekends. During the week, I'd sometimes go in late so I could work at home. Or I'd leave work early to work at home. I always tried to make my wife and daughter my first priority because they wanted me for me and not just a source of money. I always knew that it was my responsibility to support them, but I knew that no amount of money could replace my presence in their lives on a daily basis. I'm glad I did it, and I feel that my marriage and my baby show the time and effort I put into them. I know we won't have all of the luxuries that we might have if I worked harder or longer or at a different job, but I wouldn't change things at all."

Chapter Two

Depression and Rage

Most people, including mental health professionals, seem to conceptualize depression and rage as two very different entities. They view men as either sad, distant and lethargic, or else angry, quick to fly off the handle, and aggressive. I don't believe that these two concepts are mutually exclusive and, indeed, operate simultaneously in many men.

Some psychological theories have described depression as anger turned inward. These theories suggest that men find outlets for their anger or frustration over not meeting their needs, or they become angry with themselves instead of the people or circumstances that block them from meeting their needs. Anger expressed outwardly is easy to identify. It's a compelling theory and works well up to a point.

I don't agree that depression is anger focused on oneself. Other than clinical depression that may have specific genetic predispositions and is often attributed to chemical imbalances in the brain or to a specific traumatic event or series of events (e.g., assault, death of a loved one, etc.), I think that depression may act independently of anger, and that depression and rage may co-exist. In other words, sometimes anger gets activated and sometimes depression gets expressed depending on the social cues of the surrounding environment.

I believe that most men experience some level of both depression and rage, not just one or the other. I'm referring here to what is termed, sub-clinical depression, depressive symptoms that do not reach the level in the Diagnostic and Statistical Manual IV–

TR for an Axis I diagnosis. Some professionals might want to label such men as dysthymic, but each person should be evaluated on a case-by-case basis to determine the degree of depression and anger plus the thoughts, situations, and people who may be the triggers for both emotions.

It's not that men experience one emotion and not another one. They experience both simultaneously, but typically they express anger more easily than sadness. Anger is more acceptable for men to express in our society as part of the strong warrior image that is a model to follow. Furthermore, men who express anger are more easily recognizable than men who are depressed. People typically take notice of the men who act out their anger. The man who quietly moves alone through life is more likely to escape our awareness. I remember one man who described his life quite pleasantly during a beginning counseling session with me but then sighed the deepest sigh I'd ever heard. When I asked him about it and pressed him about it, he said that he felt as if he was carrying a huge load of bricks and was very tired of doing so.

I believe that men carry a level of depression and rage that has not been adequately recognized by them or by professionals. Depression is particularly underdiagnosed, I believe (Heifner, 1997). Whether anger or depression is shown overtly depends on previous learning and by the particular triggers around them.

The prior learning that shapes men into showing anger or depression usually began at home and was reinforced in social relationships. If a man saw parents who yelled and fought then he is likely to act in the same way when frustrated. Or if he saw parents who silently withdrew and acted distant then he may show the same pattern when frustrated.

The particular things that provoke the sadness or anger, could be visual, auditory or kinesthetic, all being reminders of past frustrations of the attempts to gain power or intimacy. Visual cues may include a person who reminds a man of someone from his past or photos from a high school yearbook. Auditory cues could include an old song or a baby's cry. Kinesthetic cues are those of physical sensation, such as touch or smell. Such cues could be the touch of another person or the smell of the ocean. We aren't in control of the connection between these cues or triggers and rarely know in advance when they will occur. However, the triggers need to be identified so as to reduce their power or to prevent them from provoking intense feelings without warning. Some triggers may be more likely to provoke anger, others sadness.

My goal in discussing this point is to help men and their family and friends to identify and begin to change some of these emotional conditions that allow these triggers to be so powerful. In this regard, many programs have been established for "anger management" and for "managing depression." Many of these programs use group counseling and include a systematic plan of learning about triggers in addition to cognitive and behavioral techniques to reduce the frequency and duration of the symptoms. Such plans include listing one's triggers, how to avoid them, and reduction techniques such as distraction, physical exercise, support-seeking from friends and relatives, etc. All worthwhile, however I would add the attempt to increase the awareness of the symptoms, awareness of one's feelings, and awareness of the causes of the feelings.

The problems associated with depression and rage are numerous and one must learn to recognize the signs that depict each condition. The first point is that men mask their feelings. Depressed men work very hard to put on a happy face. They never say that they feel sad or discouraged. They might go so far as to say that they're tired or even exhausted, but many men have even gotten the message that "real men don't get tired" and so can't admit fatigue. Symptoms of depressed men might include going to sleep earlier and having difficulty getting up in the morning. Another symptom might be weight gain or weight loss. Some might abuse alcohol, street drugs, or prescription medicine. The need for chemicals to help him sleep or get going in the morning is a tip-off. A significant symptom is a lack of interest in sex. Despite frequent verbal comments, jokes and bragging, men who are depressed lose interest in sex or they gain an increased interest in sex at least for a brief period of time before losing interest. Some men lose the ability to perform sexually.

Conversely, men who are angry may show a difficulty in sleeping, such as falling asleep or in waking during the night and not being able to easily fall back asleep. However, some of the nighttime wakefulness can be caused by a rebound from when the alcohol or other chemicals they took to help them fall asleep, wears off. I've often said that I could run a group for men at 4 a.m. because so many would be awake at that hour. Weight gain or weight loss would occur in some men with anger levels that reach the boiling point. Another symptom would be verbal explosions caused by seemingly minor provocations. Some men experience arguments with authorities at work or with friends during recreational activities. Disagreements about sports teams, correct golf scores, and matters that seem insignificant take on great significance. Use of drugs, alcohol or other chemicals could increase.

A common belief held by many psychologists, that I share, is that men "self-medicate" with drugs and alcohol. I think that men who feel depressed and/or angry seek to reduce these unwanted symptoms by using a substance that will reduce or calm them such as alcohol, which is very easily available and socially sanctioned by our society, or street drugs that can induce a feeling of euphoria. I remember one client who came to see me because he thought that his current Cocaine use might be blinding his judgment about marrying a woman he was currently dating, who was also a Cocaine user. We spent a long time enabling him to cope with his feelings instead of muting them with drugs.

Another point about alcohol and some drugs, but especially alcohol, is that alcohol calms a person initially (alcohol being a central nervous system depressant), perhaps after two drinks, but then for many men the chemicals reduce their social inhibitions and consequently their depression or rage emerges in full force.

Finally, the angry or rageful man may show a lack of interest in sex, but perhaps most frequently he will criticize his regular partner for not having sex often enough or not showing enough interest in sex.

Both the depressed and the angry man push others away. Although he wants just the opposite – to be approached and helped, he will distance himself because he feels so badly and can't accept help. Asking for and accepting help means that he's not a man. He rejects offers for the help that will benefit him most – a tragic irony.

As for the man who is both depressed and angry (the most common situation, I believe), he reacts in one way sometimes and one way another time depending on the circumstances around him. Sometimes he looks at himself, blames himself, and gets depressed. Other times he looks outside himself and blames others such as his parents, his wife, or his boss, and gets angry with them. The problem is that these men are difficult to relate to because they are inconsistent and unpredictable. One man with a hearing loss in couples counseling with me misunderstood what his wife said and launched into a tirade. All because he didn't hear her correctly. What he thought he heard triggered his anger.

I believe that men lack three types of awareness that keep them from making needed changes. These include: lack of awareness of their overt symptoms, lack of awareness of their feelings, and lack of awareness of the causes of either their symptoms or feelings or both.

Lack of Awareness of their Symptoms

It seems difficult to believe that people, men and women, don't identify their behavior with the same accuracy that can be easily noticed by others, yet it seems to be quite true with some, perhaps many of us. Men seem to be able to take little notice of what they say or do to those around them that often may hurt or worry others. I have heard many times in couples counseling about the husband who comes home from work, changes clothes, eats dinner and then watches television alone in the den or basement with little or no conversation with his family. When this pattern is pointed out, typical responses include: "I don't have anything to say or to ask" or "I didn't think that it bothered anyone" or "I didn't think that anyone cared what I have to say." The first response tells me, "I'm depressed." The second response says to me, "I'm too angry with you to care if I've hurt your feelings." Many men are in denial when these behaviors are pointed out and say, "I never realized I did that." And they truly don't realize what they have been doing. It just hasn't registered.

Lack of Awareness of their Feelings

As with their behaviors, men often fail to recognize how they feel, even at the moment when they are expressing very powerful feelings. I think that it's often best to assist men in gaining emotional awareness by referencing significant events in their past. Asking them how they felt when a relative or a pet died is a way to get them to establish a benchmark for other, less clear times when they experienced feelings. Asking them about a disappointment or an incident when they are likely to have felt pride, joy or fear is also a good strategy. It takes time to help them learn that they have feelings and to properly identify them.

Lack of Awareness of the Causes of their Feelings

Perhaps the most difficult of the awarenesses is the lack men have of what causes them to feel various ways. They seem not to be able to answer the "why" question; i.e., why do you feel that way? A better question is, "When and under what circumstances in the past did you feel the way you do now?" Or even, "What prompted the feelings to emerge?" This area of awareness is related to or regulated by a man's ability to reflect on himself and what causes his thoughts and feelings – something that many men lack. Some men just don't reflect on their behavior. Others can reflect but avoid doing so, perhaps being too fearful to do so.

In general, I will use these three awarenesses as a diagnostic tool when first meeting men for counseling. By assessing them on these dimensions, I know where to start and how far we need to go. These dimensions can be shared with clients and can be used in non-professional situations to get an idea how the men in your life add up.

Fear

After some time, men begin to fear, I believe, that they may never get power and/or intimacy. An irrational thought occurs that if I haven't achieved power and/or intimacy to a degree with which I'm pleased, then I may never do so. Fear can shut people down; i.e., depression, or it can make people act out; i.e., angry outbursts. It's difficult to know when and how this fear factor will emerge, but it's an added burden to the growth process and needs to be challenged. Furthermore, fear can be a motivator to encourage change, and that can propel men to seek help and advice. In some men the fear may take place when a decade birthday; e.g., turning twenty, thirty, forty, etc. takes place or when an anniversary at work happens. This brings to mind a man who told me that when he got a twenty-five year pin at his job, he knew that he had to get out and try to do what he really wanted to do in a career. Better late than never, I suppose.

Responsibility

Another part of the puzzle of whether men get depressed or enraged is their typical mode of responsibility-taking. Responsibility is a learned behavior. We learn by what is reinforced by our parents and by what is modeled by them and others for us. Some men take too much responsibility and act overly responsible. These men, I believe, are likely to be depressed. These men ignore the factors outside of themselves, such as a changing economy and changing job market or the idiosyncrasies of the people around us. Sometimes men do everything right, but the other people and conditions don't allow for much success in achieving power or intimacy.

On the other hand, some men take too little responsibility and thus act irresponsibly. These men are likely to blame others for not having sufficient power and/or intimacy and so act out their frustrations angrily.

Which is better? Neither. The best strategy, I believe, is to accept responsibility appropriately. Men should accept responsibility for the acts and decisions that were truly theirs and blame others for whatever part they played in the distress experienced. Probably, most men need to then forgive themselves for making mistakes and not beat themselves up too badly and move ahead. Similarly, men should blame others and then forgive them or at least stop blaming them and move ahead. As someone famous once said, "Stuff happens. Get over it."

A point offered by psychology is attribution bias theory. It seems that people acquire a point of view about those outside their primary social group from this primary group; e.g., family and friends. That viewpoint leads them to expect others to act in a certain way. For example, if a man hears "women can't be trusted", then he may typically distrust women with whom he comes in contact and act aloof and defensive. He attributes the characteristic of "untrustworthy" to all women and; therefore, never has much chance at intimacy. The same is true for men who see other men as aggressive and competitive. These men are likely to act aggressively in times when such behavior is inappropriate and unneeded.

Just as with the three categories of awarenesses, men need help in acting appropriately responsible. So here's the checklist for men:
- Low awareness of overt behavior to high awareness of overt behavior. High awareness is best.
- Low responsibility-taking (blaming others and things) to high responsibility-taking (blaming self for everything). Somewhere in the middle is ideal.

Acute or Chronic?

I've been assuming that men are experiencing an intense and difficult situation that they can turn around with the right kind of assistance. This assumption leads one to believe that the current depression or rage is an acute condition. Unfortunately, most men have been experiencing some level of depression and rage for quite some time, thus suggesting that their condition is chronic, needs long-term help, and has a less hopeful prognosis.

My belief is that some men have a better prognosis than others. Men who have had a longer period of frustration, poorer role models, fewer social supports, and coincidental problems of mental disorder including drug and alcohol abuse/addiction will be more difficult, but not impossible to help. Men who have had only more recently emerged symptoms; adequate prior training, social supports and a lack of coincidental problems are more likely to rapidly improve.

In the next chapters, we will examine the common patterns that men face in the struggle to achieve power and intimacy.

Chapter Three

The Exploration Phase of Early Adulthood

In my observation, exploration is the primary theme in a man's early adulthood, both in his career establishment and in the development of his social relationships. Loosening the ties to his family allows him the freedom to try out ways of working and relating. He is treated not as a son but as an adult by the world outside his parents' home. Curiosity, confidence, and idealism are high. Energy and eagerness, if insight and self-reflection are added, will make a successful explorer.

Most of the learning in early adulthood regarding power is focused on work. A man sees that the value of a job is to gain money to purchase goods and services, notably independent living; that is, housing and transportation. Many young adult men live with parents, as they can't afford to live on their own. Living with parents slows the young adult exploration process. The focus on many young adult men is to find any job that will allow them to move out of their parents' home. This pressure may lead young men to make dead-end job choices and fail, in the long run, to bring them satisfaction.

Out in the workplace, a man begins to see, often unclearly, that work is a means to achieving power as he sees other men who have achieved power through their careers. The ways to achieve power in a career are unclear and untested. Some men see the path of education or vocational training. Other men want to join with the most successful company or group of men they can find. Although the means to power may be unclear, the goal itself seems clear. The symbols of power are observed everywhere.

In the social area, a man who tries to establish friendships and have sexual relationships learns that he needs companionship, but usually does not understand the concept of intimacy. Interpersonal relationships are much less public than career activities. The means to achieve successful relationships are much less clear than the means to achieve power. Many attempts at friendships and romantic relationships will fail for a lack of understanding of what a successful relationship should entail.

The result of exploration for most men is an awareness of the importance of power. The common process of the exploration is called "trial-and-error." This means that men try a job or a relationship based on the information they choose to examine at the time and assess the results. The key is how much information men use in decision-making before they actually make a choice.

As a rule, much more information is available to them than they think to use. Two sources of information are available. One source of information about the job or relationship is external, which means the positives and negatives that are known about the job or the potential friend/dating partner. The other source of information is internal. This refers to a man's personality, intellectual and personal skills, wishes and dreams, motivation and feelings.

Unfortunately, most men at this stage of development don't do a very thorough analysis of either source of information. Why not? I think that most men don't know the process for examining the sources of information; that is, they don't know the information that's available or how to find it. Secondly, they don't think to ask others for help in seeking out or making sense of the information. It would help to have a mentor or friend with whom men could discuss these work and relationship decisions and help them do a more thorough analysis of their options.

Coworker Relationships

Although some men begin to value interpersonal relationships in early adulthood and the intimacy that may accompany them, power usually emerges at the top of the list. In other words, first they want to gain the symbols of power (primarily wealth), and then, with much less emphasis, to enjoy relationships with their coworkers and others. The emphasis in our society is to buy and consume as is described so aptly in *Culture Jam* by Kalle Lasn (1999). Lasn warns that our consumer-oriented society brainwashes people from an early age and is a very difficult grip to break.

However, the search for power should be tempered with a concern for relationships with coworkers. Research over the past 30 years shows that the main reason why workers quit jobs is that they do not get along with their boss and fellow employees. Furthermore, men who are currently dissatisfied with their job say that they do not have good working relationships with supervisors and coworkers.

Mark, age 29, is a physician in the last year of advanced training. He told me about a job opening at a prestigious hospital to which he was thinking about applying. I asked the usual questions about the tasks that would be required of him, and then inquired about how he felt about the staff members. He quickly responded, "Oh, I don't like them very much at all. They're not very friendly; sort of wrapped up in their own thing. You know, research or patient care. I'd never think of making real friends of any of them." The impact of this man's coworkers is not likely to be a positive one nor will it encourage him to behave in ways that meet intimacy needs.

At this point we began to explore how he might feel working among those people and how important it was for him to have people around him with whom he could relate in a more friendly way. He chose to go to a less prestigious setting where he liked the staff. Had this young physician not thought carefully about meeting his needs for intimacy with people at work, he might have gone through a time-consuming and painful trial-and-error process in order to reach a comfortable niche.

Even though men often quit jobs due to dissatisfaction with coworkers and/or a supervisor, they don't seem to realize that successful and satisfying coworker relationships take time and skills to achieve. Some coworkers are difficult to work with, and no one tells the young worker what to do about them.

Many men never find a job that satisfies their need for intimacy as well as their need for power. They use their job solely to acquire an apartment, clothes, and a car, and look for intimacy outside of their work place. If these men don't find intimacy outside of work, they often return to their job and work all the harder as if to try to make up for the intimacy they're missing. They often discover this error in mid-life.

Social Relationships

Outside of the work setting, the exploration of young adulthood includes spending time with friends. The friendships can provide entertainment, companionship and even intimacy. The first task is to form a set of men friends. If a man is living in the same area in which he was raised, the set of friends may already be established. The group would include those men with whom he went to high school. This is convenient but may not be as fulfilling as new connections he might find. If he lives outside his home area, he has no base on which to lean, and is forced to seek and evaluate each new relationship.

However, some men realize that they have changed since high school, and so they leave old friends behind and form new friendships with people they meet during the early adulthood exploration. As Mark, age 23, told me, "I've lost touch with some of my friends from high school, and I don't know why. I guess that we don't have that much in common any more except the things we did together in high school. I feel far away from high school now, and I suppose that means that I feel far away from them."

Another man said, "My new friends are in the same career as I am, and we like the same things; hockey, movies, weight-lifting. It seems easier to spend time with them then to call up my old high school friends who are on a very different path than I seem to be on. It's hard to explain, but it's like my high school friends and I only have the past in common, because now our interests and goals are so different. In high school our goals were just to get through school and to have fun."

The task for an early adulthood man is to meet a wide variety of people in order to determine with whom he feels comfortable in establishing intimate and lasting relationships. If he is to enjoy and cope effectively with middle adulthood then he must fully explore and evaluate relationships during this time period. He needs to learn how relationships operate. Relationships with men can provide camaraderie and support and perhaps some intimacy. Relationships with women will be complicated by the romantic aspect of the relationship.

Furthermore, relationships made now can form a support that he may carry with him through the rest of his life. To achieve an intimate relationship, a man must open up with these friends by sharing his hopes and fears with them and asking them to open up with him in return. The man who learns how to gain intimacy both in non-sexual and sexual relationships now will be prepared for future relationships.

Incidentally, men at this point in life often choose other men to be their friends rather than women. Women are not seen as friends but as dating partners. In early adulthood only the very mature man has any women friends, as most men in this exploratory stage are concerned about how they can relate to women as sexual companions. When women are seen as people to win over, they can't be seen as friends. They're part of a mating ritual, and not people in whom men can confide their inadequacies. Men believe that revealing inadequacies won't win women's attention and affection.

Paradoxically, I believe a man who has a woman friend, perhaps a sister, during this time in his life forms better relationships with dating partners than a man who doesn't have a woman friend. It helps men to have a woman's point of view, especially as it pertains to women. It's not that the woman friend is always accurate, but that she might get her male friend to have another perspective on his relationships with women. However, some patterns of behavior emerge quite typically.

Generally, men deal with their intimacy needs by resorting to three social patterns: the member of the pack, the best friend, and the half of a couple. In these situations a man can meet some of his social needs while maintaining a comfortable emotional distance.

Member of the pack

This man is part of a cluster of men, and occasionally women, who enjoy each other's companionship but are not ready to make a commitment to anyone. The group offers a chance for minimal intimacy, a little commitment, and a small amount of power (by directing the group's activities). For a few men, it's an oasis in which they unconsciously avoid the demands of a serious full-time relationship.

Martin, a pack member told me, "My friends provide me with lots of opportunities for socializing and no demands on me. The guys are the central core; but we do things with a few women friends we have and they invite us along for things too. We're all good friends. There's none of the jealousy and misunderstanding or pressure that happens with a woman you're dating."

Belonging to such a group provides a social outlet without risking serious involvement. This setting reduces the likelihood of serious relationships because people view each other primarily as pals, and it's almost taboo to become romantically involved with a group member.

For the majority of men, it's a chance to become a bit intimate with others. It's a stepping stone to more involved and committed relationships. It's a delayed adolescent stage from which men who had too little socialization in high school would profit.

Best friend

Some men can't tolerate a group. They're not comfortable with a lot of people around. These men form a solo friendship or continue a friendship from high school or college. Other men spent time in a pack and just had enough groupness. They start a friendship in the pack and then split off with that friend. The type of relationship these men establish varies from being roommates or just seeing each other frequently for recreation. They may be business partners or coworkers.

The best friend relationship was described by Kevin as, "It means always having someone to do something with. My friend Martin has ideas about what to do and where to go. I like his sense of humor and his easy-going manner. There's no pressure or strain in our relationship. I guess I like knowing that I can talk to him and that he'll be here for me. He knows that I'll help him any time and any way he asks me."

A man becomes a best friend when he is ready to have a more responsible, more intimate relationship than the pack can offer. Best friends are more likely to talk to each other when they get upset with each other. They're concerned about each other's feelings. They have made a commitment to make the relationship survive and endure, and so they continually must work out any difficulties.

The best friend is someone a man can rely on in times of economic hardship, emotional trauma or physical injury. It can provide a place where a man can discuss dating and get honest feedback. Although the friendship does not have to replace dating, it can do so.

Most men find it difficult to talk about feelings, even with a best friend. Instead, they express their feelings of intimacy non-verbally, by doing a favor, for example. They choose actions instead of words, and this can be a problem in their attempt to gain intimacy with a woman.

Half of a couple

In this pattern, a man tries to meet his need for intimacy through his relationship with a particular woman in an exclusive arrangement. A man in his twenties described his relationship as "Very important, and one that I want to keep this way forever. Denise and I do a lot together like concerts, skiing, and sometimes things with other couples, but not many parties or group stuff. I spend time at her house or else she's at my house."

The couple relationship begins to dominate a man's social life. Consequently, activities with the pack or with a best friend often decrease or stop entirely, and they may not resume until years later, if ever.

Some men, of course, skip "pack activities" or never have a best friend and go immediately into being half of a couple. Often, men who begin as half of a couple may do so precisely because they have not had a social support system, such as a pack or a best friend, to rely on for feedback and socialization. They may have chosen a couple relationship because they were needy, and a likeable woman was available. It's not a very good reason to pair up. As Dan said when he was on the way out of a couple relationship, "I moved from my parents' house right in with Cathy. I think now that it was a mistake. I need to be on my own first before I can make a relationship work."

Other men who enter a couple relationship without having a pack and best friend patterns sometimes leave the relationship years later, not knowing why they feel so restless. They may stay in the relationship and suffer in silence, making themselves and their partner miserable. Without the needed social experience and realistic feedback from social encounters, men may be headed for an unhappy relationship as half of a couple.

By contrast, men who become half of a couple and have lots of experience as a pack member and as a best friend are more likely, I believe, to have learned the necessary skills for making a relationship work. These skills include caring for another person, being reliable, offering and accepting emotional support and feedback, tolerating tension and personal idiosyncrasies, fighting fairly, and resolving conflicts quickly and efficiently. Not surprisingly, such men have the best chance for a happy, lasting marriage in my observation.

Yet, some men who have learned some lessons will fail at marriage because they accept one very deadly myth. This deadly myth is: All social needs can and should be met by one's spouse.

Somehow, as this myth commands, a man is supposed to direct all of his social needs toward his spouse. If he finds that he does have unmet social needs after being married, he must not meet these needs outside of the marriage. To do so would imply his wife is imperfect. Consequently, any outside socialization would be disloyal and unfaithful. Men must give up their friends who existed prior to marriage. This is difficult for a man to accept who only wants to go bowling on Tuesday nights. Basically, it's irrational to think that a spouse should be so perfect that he or she will meet all of a partner's needs. Sometimes men need to talk to a friend or watch a ball game with some pals. If a man, and the women he dates, maintain relationships and activities with their friends, there will be less pressure on the relationship with his dating partner to meet so many of his needs. It's a matter of keeping a dating or marital relationship from being overloaded when it's just beginning. The man who maintains men friends will cope more effectively with a dating or marital relationship.

Sexual Relationships

Questions demanding answers of early adult men include, "Am I normal to feel so sexually aroused and emotionally excited? How can I be so excited about someone I really know so little about? Does this excitement mean that I'm in love? How well should I know a woman before we have sex? Am I normal if sometimes I just care about sex and not about this woman as a friend? What does it mean when I feel obligated to this woman? Are all women like the one I'm with now? If sex did not exist, would I like to spend time with this woman?"

In early adulthood many men date, have sex, and find the whole thing confusing and frustrating. Figuring out the signals, rituals, and feelings involved is difficult. One man said, "I know that I like Diane a lot, and I want to be with her; but, I don't know if we'd be together if we weren't having sex. I guess that I should move out of my parents' house and then see how Diane and I get along when I'm on my own."

This young man must find out how to relate to women in both sexually and non-sexually intimate ways. As with men friends, the man "on his own" will find, perhaps for the first time that he is intimate with someone; that is, he's let that person behind the defensive facade that he puts on for the rest of the world. The pressure to be intimate with a lover and invulnerable to the others in his life is the beginning of a conflict that may continue unresolved for the rest of his life.

Do most early adulthood men seek sex without asking and answering many questions about sex and intimacy? Sadly, they don't consider these questions and proceed in a "trial-and-error" manner. Instead of exploration, this time becomes one of proving their masculinity to themselves in order to feel powerful.

Many men in early adulthood have sex in order to prove their masculinity, making them feel assured that they are attractive and sexually competent. Once reassured, they feel powerful.

For most men during the exploration period, sex precedes social relationships with women, just as power precedes intimacy. Relationships are likely to be brief in duration and relatively superficial in emotional intimacy. When sex becomes the reason for the interaction and because sex is designed to prove one's manhood, a relationship will have a very weak foundation. Quite typically when a man has sex to prove himself, he isn't likely to stay with one person long enough to work out an effective relationship that will make it through the long haul. Later, perhaps much later, he may feel better about himself sexually; that is, less concerned about being adequate because he truly feels adequate. Only then he can explore other aspects of being a man. In other words, once men get used to having sex, they can stop being so anxious and apprehensive about it.

Sex starts out for men as a simple, but never spoken aloud or even consciously considered, question of "Am I an adequate lover and a desirable man?" This later becomes a more complicated question as in, "How adequate and desirable am I compared to other men?" Men always move to the question of comparison. The comparison with each other usually sounds like, "I'm not adequate unless I'm as good as or better than other men are." It's clear from this thought that sex is much more than a simple physical pleasure.

As one man reported, "I never thought that sex was going to be as easy as it seems to be in movies, so I guess that I was prepared for the women I've been dating. They all seem to make me feel like I've got to be aggressive but not too aggressive, sexual but not an animal, and romantic more than anything else. I find that I think about whether I'm really doing what men are supposed to do and whether I'm doing it as well as the other men these women have had sex with."

The man who wants reassurance about his sexual adequacy has several problems. One problem is how much reassurance is enough? That is, how many women will it take to reassure him? Are two women enough or will it take 100? It depends, I believe, on the amount of the man's insecurity. Some men will never gain enough reassurance, and they'll be on a terrible search that can only be helped by a psychologist.

Another problem for men with sexual insecurity is that they see rejection of their sexual advances as a rejection of them as persons. They feel totally rejected instead of rejected for the sexual part of the relationship. Unfortunately, many men feel so rejected by a woman who declines to have sex with them that they do not continue the relationship to see what else the relationship might offer.

A sexually-rejected man, especially if rejected early and often in his encounters with women, typically withdraws and retreats from dating and sexual contact. It's tough to continue any kind of performance when he feels lousy about himself. Rejection by one or two women doesn't mean that a man is worthless, but it's tough to convince men of this idea.

A man revealed, "At the times I've been rejected by women I've asked to go to bed with me, I felt hurt and angry. If I've been nice to them in other ways when we've been dating, I think that they should go to bed with me. It's a natural development in relationships I've had with women. If I'm nice enough to go out with for a while, why aren't I nice enough to go to bed with?" It's a tough question to answer.

Some men go so far as to marry a woman during this stage of male development, largely to reassure themselves of their masculine adequacy. Unfortunately, in my view, a wife will not be able to convince these men that they are adequate. They need to understand that their sense of distress cannot be solved by a sexual relationship in which they feel powerful, but instead by understanding where their needs come from and by accepting their fears rather than denying them.

If a man is to overcome his excessive concern about his sexual adequacy then he must challenge the parental statements he learned about sex and their relationship to his adequacy. Most parents report that they said very little about "sex" to their sons, but they did act in certain ways toward each other and so modeled their views about sex. Some messages were positive and others were not. Parental messages are added to the information men get from their first-hand experience with women.

What do men learn from women about sexual relationships? Some men learn that many women need to feel secure in a non-sexual relationship before a sexually satisfying pattern can be established. A man who accepts and appreciates this fact about many women can profit from it by adopting it for himself. If a man becomes emotionally intimate before he becomes sexually intimate then he may establish a longer-lasting relationship than if sexual contact is immediately made. Many men find the rule of "Find a friend first, and then see if she can become a lover" to be very helpful.

What else do men learn about women and about themselves by means of their sexual explorations in early adulthood? Some men learn that sexual feelings can easily be confused with other feelings. Passion, tenderness, vulnerability, weakness, joy, sadness, and power are terms that have been used by men to describe their feelings during sexual encounters. Feelings seem to be linked together so that when one emotion is aroused, others are stimulated. In a highly arousing sexual encounter, a man might be surprised and confused about the variety of feelings of which he suddenly becomes aware.

One man confided, "I usually feel passionate at first and in a hurry to have intercourse once we get undressed, and then sometimes I feel aggressive, in a competitive way. And sometimes I feel evaluated or at least I wonder if the woman I'm with is evaluating me on how I'm able to make her feel. That makes me nervous."

Some men allow themselves to feel certain emotions only in sexual situations. These emotions include closeness, vulnerability, or joy. Learning to feel these emotions in non-sexual relationships will lead to increased satisfaction with life in general and make sexual relationships less complex and potentially more satisfying.

One man said, "I feel like a little boy when I have sex, sort of like protected and cared for. I never get very excited or passionate, just relaxed and gentle. I only like women who are the same way when we're in bed together. Sometimes when we're done making love, I feel like crying, not the sad kind but the happy kind."

Sexual feelings get tied up with some unpleasant feelings such as anger, rage, competition, sadness, loneliness, and fear. When sexual feelings are aroused, it's as if the lid has been lifted from a boiling pot. When a man's sexual feelings bubble out, others do too, even though the extra feelings are not always appropriate for the time and place.

Furthermore, some men who feel incompetent or inadequate in non-sexual areas such as work try to feel better by having sex. The image of the sexually active man is a powerful one in our society and one that many men use to make themselves feel better. If men could reduce their use of sex to compensate for a feeling of powerlessness and instead try to feel more intimate, they would find, I believe, that the integration of the two needs would lead to a more satisfying sexual relationship.

One man described, "I first never felt anything toward the women I became sexually intimate with except love. Maybe I had to fall in love with a woman before I could have sex with her. Later I realized that I felt powerful and fulfilled, like accomplishing something important."

Men need to learn that dating and sexual relationships can produce more than companionship and sexual satisfaction, but they need to understand much more about power and intimacy before they can satisfy these two needs.

Marital Relationships

Some men marry during the exploration period of early adulthood, and the statistics on divorce suggest that these men make a big mistake. These men believe a fantasy about relationships and need a larger dose of reality before they attempt to establish a lasting marriage. Some of these men seek, I believe, to be more powerful and others seek intimacy, but are not fully aware of how these needs are motivating them.

I believe that the need for power is reflected in the man who says that he wants to get married because he's "ready." Very often he wants to marry because of a desire to be accepted as a more fully-functioning adult member of society. Society clearly conveys that married people are more responsible than single people. Responsible people have gained a greater status in society, and status is power.

A man confided to me, "I know that I haven't dated too many girls besides Pat, but I really love her. I want to spend all of my free time with her and do things with her, even boring things like errands. I'd say that we have a great relationship." Another man reported, "I'm ready to be married and settle down, I'd say. I've had enough running around, and I'm tired of it. A regular life is what marriage means to me." This awareness of being a single person and not yet being a complete adult is a strong motivator for young men to marry.

It is clear to me that some men marry so they won't feel so doubtful about their lack of power at work, with their parents, or about sex. They believe that marriage will allow them status within the community and allow them to feel powerful with another person. These men may harbor a deep sense of inadequacy. Somehow they perceive that a wife will provide the reassurance that they desire.

Other men marry to meet a need for intimacy that has begun to be met during a courtship. Dating provides an ideal time for laying the groundwork for intimacy. I believe that levels of intimacy exist depending on how open a couple can be with each other and how much each person knows about himself/herself. The more exploration and reflection on that exploration, the more a couple can gain the highest levels of intimacy. For example, at beginning levels of intimacy, couples learn about their preferences and aversions in music, clothing, and leisure activities, to name a few areas. At intermediate levels they know each other's levels of frustration, motivations, and values. At higher levels they know the other person's fears, doubts, and wounds. As openness increases, the façade is pushed back. The process is helped by people who are open to exploration, who have information on hand to provide and who can provide the information willingly.

Dating relationships in early adulthood may not move beyond the beginning levels of intimacy. I don't believe that a marriage can survive with intimacy being met at only these lower levels. Marriages will suffer lots of challenges, and they require high levels of intimacy in order to survive. The challenge for men in the exploration phase is to understand the levels of intimacy that exist and to attempt to reach them with their future wife before the marriage ceremony.

Integrating Power and Intimacy

Perhaps the most important idea to keep in mind is that trying out different jobs and different relationships is appropriate and valuable. Each man should explore the fantasy about work acquired from his parents or from other sources. In addition he must experience his fantasy about friends and lovers. By letting himself enter relationships with people from a wide range of backgrounds and with different personalities, interests, and values, he is likely to discover people with whom he can feel both powerful and intimate.

Experiencing power often leads men to want more. Should a man see other men search for power to the exclusion of intimacy only to realize how hollow and insecure they really are, then he may be able to move away from that search himself.

One man recalled, "I remember being very competitive when I was growing up. I was out to win at athletics and with women. Then one day all of a sudden, I started to look at the guys in college who were the big shots. I saw, somehow, that they were really phony and only cared about themselves. The only friends they had were people who were trying to make themselves look good by associating with the big guys. I realized that I didn't want to pretend to be something more than what I was. I wanted to see if people would like me if they really knew me. I found out that some people would and some wouldn't. I started to get close to people and be open with them. Oh, I could still get competitive at sports sometimes but not in a casual game of softball or cards. It just didn't matter anymore."

Similarly, experiencing intimacy can lead to wanting more. Because men understand so little about intimacy, they often have few chances of experiencing intimacy, let alone integrating intimacy with power in their relationships.

Men who achieve intimacy tend to balance power and intimacy in their twenties and thirties, rather than integrate the two. By "balancing", I mean that they have some relationships in which they feel powerful, perhaps at work, and some relationships in which they feel intimate, perhaps with spouse and family. These men alternate when their needs are met, rather than having some of both needs met in the same relationship. On a scale of mental health, isolation (seeking only power or only intimacy) would be on the low end, balancing or alternating would be in the middle, and integration would be at the top. It's a process through which men can move if they see the direction and work at it.

Chapter Four

The Transition to Thirty

Introduction

During early adulthood, usually the twenties, men begin to believe that they might not have as much power and intimacy (however, they may define it) as they want or think that they should have by this stage in life. The end of any period in which they wish they'd have done more or had done things differently brings disappointment. It's no wonder that men want to avoid examining their lives at thirty. Nevertheless, denying their feelings won't help for very long.

Men have been influenced by the negative messages that they have received from advertisements, movies, songs, and books. These negative messages include that: a) men are no longer "young" when they hit thirty and b) men must have made significant personal and career achievements by the time they turn thirty. Consequently, men believe a cultural myth that is not true.

No longer "young"

The damaging part of this message is that "young" is viewed as being better than "old." Therefore, many men believe that men who are no longer "young" are somehow less powerful and no longer as valuable as they once were. It's a terribly inaccurate statement because men over thirty have tremendous power and influence, which often increases as men move through their thirties and forties and far beyond. Nevertheless, many men believe that over 30 is "old", and "old" means powerless.

The basis of this myth may be that men attach their self-evaluation to their physical ability. Certainly, men in their late twenties may not be able to match their athletic abilities of their early twenties and teens. I've always suspected that men who continue to play basketball or soccer in adulthood did so for more reasons than physical fitness. Maintaining a fantasy of athletic prowess may ward off disappointments about lacking power in other areas.

A second basis for concern for men approaching thirty is that they are not as attractive as they once were due to weight gain, hair loss, declining vision and the need to wear glasses, and so forth. If they are no longer attractive then they may have lost the power to attract women and to keep a woman, such as a wife, attached to them.

Real men make it by thirty

Many men react to "You should have gotten it by thirty" with a fear that they will never get what they want if they haven't achieved it by now. At the same time, they feel pressured by the younger men on the job and on the social scene. Some men react to this pressure by grabbing the symbols of achievement at the expense of the credit limits of their charge accounts.

A new car, an apartment, nice clothes, a good job, and an attractive girlfriend or wife are some of the symbols that a successful man is supposed to acquire by thirty, and many men feel compelled at this time to flaunt that fact that they are "making it." Many men in my experience who lack these status symbols feel very upset about it.

It's no wonder many men feel anxious when age thirty nears. As George, a married man with kids, who is successful, and seemingly content, reported, "I wasn't bothered by turning thirty until three weeks before the big day. And then I felt depressed to the point of suicide." Of course, men at thirty still have an excellent chance for success and happiness, but even those who made some clear choices about a career and a stable and reliable lifestyle can start to feel doubtful about themselves when they near thirty.

At the same time social life, in many respects, is not quite as new and enthralling as it had been. The excitement of "playing the field", for example, has faded. By now, the sexually active man has satisfied his curiosity and may realize the difference between sexual and interpersonal intimacy, or as some men have put it, the difference between "making love and being in love." As Dan, the young attorney, disclosed to me, "It's less intimate and much less threatening to me, to have sex with a woman than to kiss her. But even though it makes me nervous, I'd rather feel that I was having a significant relationship than a sexual orgy."

Many men no longer feel so bullish about their sexual prospects. By now most men have had a serious relationship fall apart. Others feel disappointed that they meet only women who "aren't right" for them. No longer are they so sure that relationships are easy. No longer are they confident that they can become involved with a woman and still feel in control. No longer do they assume that they can receive comfort from a woman without doing much in return.

This reality in combination with the disappointments in their career and social life can propel many men to outgrow their adolescent self-absorption and start yearning for substance and meaning. It's no longer enjoyable for them to date every night of the week, to throw themselves into weekend romances, and to work at jobs just to receive a check. Typically, men are drawn at this age to activities that reflect the beginnings of mature choice, greater orientation toward the future, and an increased sense of responsibility for the feelings of others. These activities may lead to more effective ways of gaining long-term power and intimacy.

One active socializer told me, "Parties and group activities are rare occasions now. Everyone's dating someone, and they're out together or maybe with another couple. It's a real couples' world." Another man said, "The pressure to find someone and settle down is really there. No one says anything to you, but when all your buddies are dating someone and you can't get together with them, you feel the pressure." One other man said rather sadly,

"Dating's fine, but you've got to get serious. You have to decide if this person's right for you. I thought Mindy was right for me, but it didn't work out. Now I'm really careful about dating women who don't look like they're the serious type."

At this phase in life, the myth that they must achieve power and intimacy by age thirty teaches many men that they must get serious about their career and their social life.

The Transition

Until thirty, it's acceptable to explore, travel, date casually, or hop from job to job. After thirty, society (at least those people in society over the age of thirty) expect men to stop challenging authority, wasting time in exploratory jobs, and dating women with no intention of a serious relationship. Men are supposed to become stable in both their career and personal relationships whether they're ready or not.

One group of men hears this message clearly during their twenties and so prepares themselves by means of a careful and thoughtful search of jobs and relationships. These men make the thirties transition a slow and steady one with little turmoil, although they may not be completely satisfied with how they have met their needs for power and intimacy. These reflective men, perhaps after some period of depression, move forward again, maybe with a new job and a new wife, but forward none the less.

A second group of men plunges ahead with the strength of will that carries them through any obstacle. They have enormous energy and confidence in their abilities to achieve their dreams. They may be men who started later than others and so charge onward with energy generated by fear of not catching up. They could be early-starters who always have been on the fast-track, perhaps due to fear that they'll be caught from behind. Unfortunately, all of these men pay little attention to the physical or emotional signs around them that give other men time to reflect and reassess.

Men who ignore the opportunity to pause at thirty for a review of their lives often have a tough time at forty or sometime later, I've observed. A forties crisis could be diminished or eliminated, I believe, if these men would slow down during the transition to thirty and evaluate where they are and how much it's cost them to get there. Sometimes it takes a crisis, such as a life-threatening illness, accident, or the death of a friend or family member to cause them to consider their lives.

One man stopped short at thirty because he ran out of goals. He was educated, socially skilled and hard-working. He accomplished by thirty what other men might have accomplished by forty. He got depressed three weeks before his thirtieth birthday because he had nowhere left to go (or so he thought). He felt burned out and scared because he had accomplished the life goals that he had set years before. He could see no future because his need for power had been met. After some time and reflection, he established new goals, such as helping younger people in his field, as well as seeking greater intimacy with his family.

Like many men, this man also had to stop feeling disloyal about exceeding the life achievements of his father and his mentors from college. He finally accepted that his father and mentors were truly proud of his accomplishments and not resentful of his going beyond them. Once he realized that his achievements wouldn't alienate him from the people he cared about, he was able to resume his life.

A third group of men hit thirty with surprise and distress. It's quite likely that they heard the message decades ago but didn't want to think about it or worry about it. These men convinced themselves that the freedom of early adulthood would last forever. Everything is fine for these men who ignore society's message until the first job rejection by an employer who wants someone younger or a rejection by a woman who wants someone more serious.

Men who charge through the transition at thirty to avoid the disappointment of their twenties are so anxious about the future (or disappointed about the past) that they live years ahead of themselves. Men who approach thirty so intensely involved in a life plan often miss the valuable opportunity to assess the past and adjust their plan, which would normally include intimacy.

One important question for these men to ask themselves is, "What significant relationships do I have that are readily available to me and that I can count on in a pinch?" Many men, especially married men, are unable to list any friends except their wives, which is a special case.

Some men list a few people, but upon closer scrutiny it's clear that they don't meet with or talk to these "friends" very often and certainly don't talk openly with them. Men think that they have friends when, many times, they really only have acquaintances.

One man reported to me, "When Don got married, he chose someone else to be his best man. I always assumed from high school that we'd be the best man for each other at our weddings. Maybe I misjudged him, or maybe he's changed, and I haven't noticed it." This man, and others like him, has too few resources to help him through the struggles of the coming decades. He'll need all the support he can find.

While jogging together by chance one day, a man opened up to his neighbor for the first time. They never jogged together again. Perhaps they avoided contact because they were not ready or able to feel comfortable with supporting each other. In a different pair of joggers, one man opened up to the other and at the conclusion of the run and the discussion, they agreed to talk to each other whenever they were under pressure and needed a listener. When I asked the listener in this dyad if he would reciprocate and open up in the future as his comrade had done, the man responded, "No way!" It's not easy for men to find support and a reciprocal relationship among other men.

Career Reality

Many men realize that although they have the skills and training for a particular career field, they just aren't having their needs met. The task for most men is to make a choice that will be appropriate for their abilities and be satisfying enough to sustain them for the next decade and beyond.

Scott (twenty-nine years old and married with two small children) said, "Every day I go to work, I can't wait to leave. I have trouble remembering the features of the products and what they're used for. I often forget price changes. It feels like I struggle to sell things while the other salespeople around me do it easily." I asked how he felt when he'd had a good sales day. He replied, "Oh, I'm happy that I sold a lot, but more so that I didn't get hassled by so many people as I usually do. I don't feel that my high sales total was something that anyone else couldn't have done."

I questioned him about the most enjoyable aspect of his job. Scott related, "I guess I only like it when customers are friendly and polite. Whether they buy items or not is separate. I know that it seems that I can't take rejection. It sounds like I personalize customers' not wanting to buy something. Maybe I do."

Later he added, "I like working with customers, but I don't like pressuring them to buy something that they don't really need. I feel guilty because I talked them into buying a vacuum cleaner or something, even though my supervisor wants me to do precisely that. Sometimes customers don't realize that they could do just fine with a broom." This reluctant salesman sounds as if he has the technical skills but his need for pleasant relationships with customers makes job satisfaction and possibly success at his present job seem questionable.

Charles, a twenty-five year old social worker who is married with two children said, "Social work has become frustrating and disappointing to me. There aren't enough funds, too much red tape, and clients who are just not motivated. I've gotten more and more disillusioned about how I can make even a little difference." I asked him about "making a difference."

He went on to elaborate. "I want to know that my being here on earth has been worthwhile, that I had an impact on someone or something. I'd like to be a Senator or Mayor for a while and see what I could do. But I know that I wouldn't really want to campaign and run for office."

I inquired about what other job he might find that would satisfy his needs. He wondered aloud with a great deal of confusion. "I'm really unsure what I could do. Maybe go into a business with products or services that people really needed. Maybe be a lawyer for people with low incomes or maybe the ministry." This dissatisfied social worker may have the skills for the job, but his need for power is unmet. Like the reluctant salesman, this man needs a change.

Most men seek a career that offers them the satisfaction of their power need, and then hope they have time to meet their intimacy need. If they can't meet their power need, they usually bury the need for intimacy deeply within them until they can find a career. This gives them suitable power or they find a different way to meet their need within their present job. It's as if they can't focus on satisfying two needs simultaneously. Several patterns emerge that depict the man who suffers dissatisfaction of his need for power in his career.

The majority of men change jobs and even their career field until they find the one that meets their need for power. It takes time, but now is the time to do it. Searching is far better than staying stuck.

Some men ignore their vague feelings of dissatisfaction and refuse to try out a new career. They stay stuck in a rut, too scared to try something more satisfying, or too intimidated by a parent who pressured them into the particular career, or too obligated to carry out the provider/protector role because they married before they had completed a sufficient career exploration. Little do these men realize that when they're forty, they may feel so powerless that they'll experience a mid-life crisis that will bring immense pain and suffering.

Other men choose a second and a third career that are just as dissatisfying as the earlier ones. This pattern of repeating their errors in judgment causes them to forego their needs for intimacy even further. These men seem to make poor decisions repeatedly without learning from their previous errors. Men who are stuck in a single job and those who are stuck in a pattern of random job-hopping must seek assistance. They could benefit from vocational testing, counseling, and career planning. These men need to know their career strengths and weaknesses, their interests, and information about the requirements and rewards of various careers.

Both Scott, the salesman, and Charles, the social worker, received the help they needed and went on to change career fields. Scott went into social work and Charles went into government service as an administrator in a veteran's administration hospital with a lot of patient contact.

In contrast to the men who struggle to establish themselves, there are highly independent free spirits who work as artists, ski instructors, and waiters. They're mavericks who usually have no obligations such as wives and mortgages. It's a cowboy image that's such a romantic part of our culture.

Most of these men do settle down. Eventually, they begin feeling a need for intimacy, and so they seek a mate, which then leads them into a job with security and stability. Gradual settling is their method, and it takes a long time. They haven't lost out by taking this time. As one of my clients described it, "Some people take a different path than others do."

Whether men are disappointed with their career choice or pleased about it, whether they choose a career with insufficient exploration or they postpone making a choice for a decade or more, eventually most men learn valuable lessons about themselves as they approach thirty. Of the lessons that most men learn, the first one is that they do not excel at everything. They excel in certain areas and not others. This may come as a shock to the man who hasn't been out in the working world very much.

The typical problem occurs when a man learns that he's not very strong in an area in which he thought he would be. One client of mine remembered a conversation in which his boss at the gas station told him "Mike, you're really good with people. I mean the sales part, but not at mechanical repairs. Have you considered a different kind of job?" Despite the hardships, trial and error is an excellent, but time-consuming, way to learn about one's skills.

The second lesson that most men learn in their approach to thirty is responsibility. Responsibility in a career means taking on tasks that require independent decisions and good judgment, completing tasks without being supervised, punctuality, and reliability.

By the end of the reality period, many men learn to be responsible and to accept the limits of their abilities within their careers. Social life is another part of life in which early adulthood men experience reality -- and learn from it.

Social Reality

By now the single man between the ages of 28 and 32 has moved out of his parents' house and has suffered the ending of at least one romantic relationship. Perhaps he lived with one or two women. He thinks he knows what kind of woman would be right for him, but he just can't seem to meet her. He may not have many opportunities to encounter women without taking energy away from his career search. Serious dating takes time and energy.

Here's the crossroads for the single man in the transition to middle adulthood. He asks himself, "Should I satisfy my need for power by concentrating on my career or should I meet my need for intimacy by searching for that special woman?" Should he spend time on intimacy then he fears that he may delay finding an acceptable career, or that he may not advance as rapidly in the career he already has chosen. On the other hand, if he throws himself into his career then he fears that he won't find a mate and thus will feel detached and lonely.

Searching in earnest

The man at thirty who seriously looks for a mate will make all sorts of changes. He may join a therapy group, learn how to ski, exercise more, and seek out single women through the Internet. Paradoxically, this man will have trouble if he uses these tactics for gaining power in the search of intimacy. He may believe that good things happen to those who work hard, but he may be using the wrong strategy.

The problem with the methodical searcher is that his spontaneity is buried. Women become leery when they sense that they're being evaluated closely. A single man must seek someone who would make a good mate without appearing to be too serious or anxious about his search. If he looks too intense, he'll appear desperate or dependent or both. It's a difficult paradox in which to be caught.

I believe that men must give up some of their excessive responsibility-taking and give themselves a break. They must realize that they can't control all of the factors in dating and interpersonal relations, and stop trying so hard. Once men see the struggle as a control issue of their own doing (with the help of society), they can let go a little. As with many issues, men try too hard to control aspects of their lives that are uncontrollable.

The conscientious searchers should extend the time limits of their search indefinitely. They shouldn't abandon the search in a gloom of disappointment after some predetermined time period. They should attend social gatherings and host social gatherings. It's difficult to be disappointed and keep on going, but that's exactly what needs to be done. Intimacy cannot be achieved as methodically as a man gains power.

A different concern that some men have at the transition to thirty is that they're dating a woman and the relationship isn't working out. It's a relationship that isn't good enough to warrant marriage, but it's not bad enough to end. This man wants companionship and intimacy and so he won't give up his current partner until he finds or stumbles upon a replacement. He may also be anxious about being alone. The intimacy that he has with his current partner is enough to keep him in the relationship even though he's quite disappointed. He may also fear the guilt of causing his partner the pain of a break-up. It may appear that he's "leading her on", but he's really just avoiding the pain of being honest. Waiting for a "replacement" is not a good strategy, in my opinion.

First of all, the man in a relationship that isn't heading for marriage who meets a new woman must go through a break-up with his current partner at the same time that he's trying to establish a new relationship. People who are ending a relationship are distressed and are not at their best. Furthermore, the new woman will wonder if she's being used as a vehicle to escape a relationship that this man couldn't end on his own. I believe that it's in a man's best interest to end one relationship before he searches for a new relationship.

How long should a man spend in a new relationship to see if it's likely to meet his needs? After six months of dating a particular woman exclusively, the majority of men, in my experience, know if they want to move toward marriage with her or not. If they have discussed their most intimate beliefs about relationships such as money, children, lifestyle, religion, and values then the relationship has proceeded beyond the dating stage to the seriously-getting-to-know-you stage. If a man feels sufficiently powerful in the relationship and sufficiently intimate also, then the relationship is likely, I believe, to move toward marriage. Power in the relationship often means a man is able to influence his partner in making plans affecting both of them and feels as if he can control a certain part of his leisure time. Intimacy in the relationship frequently means feeling attractive to his partner and emotionally supported by her.

On the other hand, if a man hasn't gotten past the dating stage after six months, then, I believe that it is doubtful that he will ever do so with this woman. Often men feel pressured by their partner and fear they may fail at delivering what the partner wants. Or they don't perceive that their partner's care will last. He must either leave or accept a relationship that has little chance for becoming full-time (marriage or living together). Full-time relationships have the greatest chance for fulfilling needs, but if a man can't take the risk for the full-time commitment then a part-time commitment will suffice as long as both partners agree to it.

Avoidance through work

Some single men approaching thirty have had significant disappointments in their relationships with women and feel hesitant to try again. These men often turn toward their work as a source of satisfaction to replace the satisfaction of interpersonal relationships. The man who turns toward work may receive rewards for his efforts. He may acquire additional education, make a career shift, or start a part-time business. He may apply himself so industriously to his work that he moves up rapidly in his company.

He also may work in his community through civic projects, political campaigns, or church organizations.

But will feeling powerful compensate for a lack of intimacy? I do not believe so. This avoidant man may feel good about himself through accomplishments, but that's very different than feeling good about himself through social relationships. For healthy psychological development, I believe, men must feel satisfied by attaining power and by attaining intimacy. One area can never fully or adequately compensate for the other. The man who avoids the pain of dating by working may successfully avoid the pain for a while, but it will arise later, even years later.

Married at thirty

Here's a man approaching thirty. He's been married for three to seven years and is concerned about saving to buy a house or about paying for the one he's already bought. He has a young child, a job, and worries he never thought about before marriage. He wants to know about school systems, parks, taxes, security from crime, and facilities for shopping. He feels a lot of responsibility for other people. The pressure of responsibility may be too much, or it may have come too soon. In addition a man may not have learned how to sacrifice some of his needs for the needs of others.

The pressure of responsibility grows throughout a man's lifetime but in an uneven manner. In early adulthood it can change significantly, virtually overnight, from being single and working in an exploratory job to being married, a father, and a relied-upon coworker. It's the suddenness of the change and the amount of change from carefree youth to responsible adult that's upsetting to many men, regardless of the chronological age at which this change takes place.

At work a man often says, "If I don't do my part then others will suffer." A man revealed, "I've got to come up with the right answer because the project depends on it. I don't want to let my coworkers down or the clients either. I'd feel guilty." Another scenario is "I've got to meet the sales quota or I'm not going to move up. I don't want to be stuck at this salary forever. I want more for my family."

At home it may be a case of "I want to be a good husband, but I never imagined that my wife would ask so much of me." Many men are asked to share in household chores including non-traditional tasks such as cooking, cleaning, and laundry as well as infant care. They also may be asked to give advice, emotional support, and care for in-laws. These tasks can be overwhelming depending on how prepared a man is to respond to these requests.

Responsibility feels like a suit that a man only wears on Sunday. It's the right size, but he's not used to the feel of it. Getting used to the feel of responsibility is important if a man is to take on the societal roles that lie ahead. At the most basic level the competence question arises; that is, "Can I meet the demands that are placed on me?" Some say, "Yes, I'm willing to try and then I'll know", while others say "No, I don't want to find out, so I'm leaving." Others seem to say, "I'll be very responsible at work but not at home. I need a break." The fear of not being competent enough is a big factor in many decisions that they will face each day.

When men are faced with society's demands that responsibility be shouldered, they cope with their fear, conscious or unconscious, that they may not be powerful enough to carry out these tasks successfully. The result of failure would be a loss of ego; that is, a sense of powerlessness and disappointment. Some men decide to evade society's influence and leave marriage and fatherhood rather than face failure in that area.

Mark said, "All of a sudden, I looked around and realized that Jeanne and I had joined some couples who went to a football game each weekend in the fall and then out for pizza at the same restaurant. One or two Saturday nights each month we played Bridge with them. I had a secure high school teaching job and Jeanne's job was secure too. I think the thing that shook me up was in the church we were about to join; the minister left his wife and ran off with one of members of the congregation. Somehow, escape sounded pretty good. I had bigger dreams than could be fulfilled in that town." Escape (or change) is the answer of some men to the questions, "Where am I at thirty? How do I feel about it? And if I'm unhappy about it, what am I going to do about it?"

The second factor, in my opinion, in determining the success of marriage as men approach thirty is if they can sacrifice (as they view it) or change their desire to meet their own needs first and in their own way of doing so. Men often see that taking less or waiting for what they want is a failure. Their image of being masculine gets tied into getting what they want and when they want it. The underlying issue is power. In other words, men believe that a man who can get his needs met is truly a man and that equals power. Sacrifice and compromise feel like impotence. I suspect that this explains why some men feel anxious and even angry when they wait in a line at a restaurant.

At home the conflict feels like, "If I satisfy myself then my wife will be upset." Many men put social situations into an "either you or me" category in which two people cannot have their needs fulfilled simultaneously. It's a classic "win-lose" power struggle; that is, if a man has his needs met when he wants and how he wants then he wins. If he doesn't then he loses. That's how many men feel in their marriage, but it doesn't have to be that way.

One man revealed how his desire to buy a motorcycle made this conflict clear to him. He said, "I realized that the motorcycle was a toy and a way to hang on to some of my youth. Linda was so worried about my getting hurt or killed and leaving the baby and her alone that I just couldn't buy it. I'm not mad. I'm sad. At that moment I realized that I would be sacrificing my own needs for theirs for the rest of our lives."

Some men compound the struggle at home by establishing the discussion in the form of their needing to relax after a tiring job. As one man stated, "I really want to come home and read the paper after work. But Sue wants to talk to me about her day. I can't concentrate on her then, and she feels rejected and hurt. I don't know what to do." I think that many men use this "need to relax" request as a way to avoid the responsibility of home and family tasks that may be as disappointing as the tasks they have experienced at work. Naturally, their way of relaxing is a solitary form in which there is no social contact with their wives. Going to the gym, reading, napping, or listening to music or watching television are fine as long as they are not an avoidance of the responsibilities of home and an escape from the request of intimacy. These men may need to cope more effectively with feelings of anxiety and/or disappointment about work that make it difficult for them to take on more responsibility at home.

A word about fatherhood is important here because men sometimes feel that they give up their needs in order to meet the needs of their child. This may be true for some men who feel their power diminish when children arrive, but it is possible for a man to feel the power of interpersonal influence when interacting with his children. He's one of the most powerful and influential people in his children's lives. For fulfilling intimacy needs, children are extremely open about their feelings, which allows men to be open with them. Going to the park or to the hardware store provides an opportunity to gain intimacy if only men would perceive the chance and then take it.

Young fathers seem to have difficulty getting past the drudgery to get to the parts that can satisfy their needs for power and intimacy. Will changing diapers ever be fun? Probably not. Will cleaning up Blueberry Buckle (a favorite baby dessert) from the walls and floor ever be pleasant? Not likely.

A man needs to transform "her versus me" or "win-lose" choices into "us" or "both win" interactions. It's not easy to accept sacrifice, but he must realize that his wife's request is a statement of how important he is to her. Second must come the idea that new ways of meeting needs might be just as effective as the old ways. Third must come the realization that withdrawing from a power struggle of who does more or gets more increases the chance for intimacy.

Career at home or at the office

Many men face a lifestyle that includes a wife who works full-time. Her career is at an office and not at home. For a traditional man this lifestyle requires a change in expectations and behavior.

Carl works outside the home and his wife, Julie, does too. They have a son who is eight months old. Carl wants Julie to stay at home with their son, but feels that he shouldn't tell Julie what to do with her life. He feels that it might be better for their relationship and for the raising of their son if Julie worked instead of staying home and became resentful of doing so. He thinks that Julie wants to be a superwoman. Although Julie is good at her job and good at being a mother, Carl fears that she may be burning out. No one can be great at everything, especially when the demands of career and child-raising are so steep, thinks Carl.

Their neighbors, John and Sarah, both work outside their home, but Sarah is unhappy about spending so little time with their one-year-old daughter. John wants Sarah to be happy, but he feels a lot better about paying their bills with the help of Sarah's income. He wouldn't like to carry the whole economic burden, and he'd resent Sarah for "wasting" her education and skills and neglecting to help him with the financial part of their lives.

Neighbors down the street, Jerry and Ann, both work outside their home and have a son who is about 14 months old. Ann, like Sarah, wants to stay at home more with her son, but knows that Jerry wouldn't like that. Jerry met Ann when they both worked for the same company, and he was impressed with her intelligence and competence. Ann fears that she would lose some of her appeal to Jerry as "just a housewife"; which is the role Jerry's mother played when he was growing up.

Each of these three couples has a similar challenge. They all need to discuss their wishes and concerns openly with each other. They need to change their expectations or change their lifestyle in order to make their relationship last. How can these men feel powerful and intimate in their lives if their marital relationship doesn't deal with the issues that face them? Some couples feel that another child is the answer.

Another child

Unfortunately, some men have a second child in order to compensate for needs for power and intimacy that are unmet in their marriage. These unmet needs play out in several scenarios.

One man wants a second child in hopes that a child will draw his wife closer to their home and closer to him. He may hope that the child will force his working wife to stay home. Two children, he thinks, are more likely to keep her at home than one child did. The issue of having a working wife may disappear if his wife stays home with the two kids, but the underlying issue of his feeling a diminished sense of power in the face of his wife's competence and assertiveness won't disappear after a second child arrives. The feelings surrounding this issue will diminish the intimacy that they have established between them unless they begin to talk about it.

Another man wants a second child so that he and his wife will have something to share and to be intimate about as they did with their first child. If this couple only feels close when a child is born, they have a problematic relationship.

Some men resist having a second child because they fear the increased financial pressure and child-raising responsibilities. Other men fear that a child might take away the time they now have with their wives. Couples who seek help specifically about this concern always need to work on their relationship in order to decide whether or not to have a second child. When the fears of the father are reduced or their ways of achieving intimacy are expanded, then they can make a more reasonable decision.

Using the same old strategy

One characteristic of Western society is men's increased specialization in work. When men become specialists or experts at work, they believe that they know so much that they can predict what will happen under various conditions and, somehow, control the future. Many men during the transition to thirty period often work to control their future. Many men believe that if they work harder or longer in their career that they will be successful eventually. It's as if they believe that, "Hard work is always rewarded." Unfortunately, men who follow this strategy often fail to see ways to do their work faster and easier, especially by means of more effective relationships with the boss and their coworkers.

A young attorney spent ten to twelve hours a day at work in the firm in which he was a partner. There was too little time for his wife (also an attorney), his child, his friends, recreation, or exercise. Eventually, he started to work less and began to have more time with friends and family.

He stopped being such a "cog in the wheel" and started to be more creative, much more of an individual, and more friendly to those around him at work, from colleagues to secretaries. Previously, he had believed that by narrowing his focus to work exclusively, or almost exclusively, that he would be more successful. It's difficult to try a new strategy instead of using the same old one.

Men who can't change their ways of relating to their work have problems changing their ways of relating to wives and kids. For some reason they do the same things over and over even though it makes their relationship with their wives and kids more strained.

A man yelled at his wife for making errors in their personal checkbook and in his business checkbook (he's self-employed, operating out of the home). She told him to hire someone to do the books or do it himself, but he refused. After she moved out for six weeks, he stopped being upset over the checkbook and hired a bookkeeper for a few hours each month. He thought that his wife had not been concentrating hard enough and that if he yelled loud enough and often enough that she would realize how important it was to him. He was completely wrong. He failed to realize that she wasn't skilled at math and was tired from taking care of their kids.

Another man did few chores around his home and focused on his career. This man's son came to the brink of failing out of high school and his wife became seriously depressed. The more he worked, the worse they got. He thought that if they recognized how hard he worked then they would eventually let him alone. They didn't and got even worse.

Changing to a new approach means admitting that something's wrong and, by implication, that a man failed at the first approach that he used. This is the view that makes it difficult for many men to try a new approach.

Going it alone

The transition around thirty often witnesses the end of friendships that lasted since high school, college or the service. It seems that marriage, children and job responsibilities pull men away from their friendships. I believe that these men don't take the time to keep up their relationships with their men friends primarily because they don't see the rewards that these friendships can provide. Men see women maintain their friendships with other women but men don't seem to follow this example.

Some men have friends who are women. I asked a group of ten psychologists at a convention to identify their best friend. None of them named a man. Some of the married men named their wives, and when asked for a second choice they named a woman or no one at all.

Men who choose women friends do so, I believe, for several possible reasons. One reason may be that men feel safe with women. Other men are seen as their primary competitors. A second reason is that men who plan a lunch meeting or a tennis game with a man friend start to feel that the planning and the activity itself is too much like a date. Dating is what men do with women. Dating a man would seem too homosexual and that is an impression that heterosexual men wish to avoid creating. Furthermore, if men start to enjoy a caring and open relationship with a man friend then they may start to confuse the feelings of intimacy confused with sexual feelings.

Men who choose women as friends are likely, in my opinion, to deal with sexual feelings that often surface. The power concept of winning a sexual prize overwhelms the need for an intimate friendship. Usually men break off a friendship with a woman rather than admit to having sexual feelings. If they do admit to having these feelings, they act on them rather than talk about them. Unfortunately, men seem to treat a potential woman friend exactly like a girlfriend. They try to have sex with her or else drop her completely. Many men haven't learned that they can treat a woman as a friend without having sex interfere. Only by de-sexualizing a relationship with a woman friend can the need for intimacy be met.

In order for men to "de-sexualize" their relationship with a woman whom they want to make their friend, they must talk to her about any sexual feelings and fantasies that they possess toward her. If a man talks openly about his sexual feelings with his woman friend then he gradually gains control over these feelings. Additionally, she becomes less of an idealized object and more of a real person with qualities (other than sexual) that are of value. Open conversation allows the feelings to become attached to a more suitable person.

Why do sexual feelings appear in the first place? As a man approaches a woman he becomes somewhat vulnerable. As she accepts him, he feels closer to her. Closeness or intimacy, in men, is synonymous with sexual feelings. Sexual feelings will stay in the way until the man separates sexual feelings from intimacy.

Ethan reported this interchange to me, and I think it summarizes his difficulty with talking about his feelings very well. Ethan had been confiding in a woman about his best friend, Danny. Ethan's confidant said, "Why don't you talk to Danny? You and he used to be the closest of friends." Ethan replied, "I don't know. It's like we're prisoners locked inside ourselves." Men who expand their narrow focus to friendships with others may be able to unlock themselves and begin to live more satisfying lives. The transition around age thirty is an excellent time to move toward intimacy with others.

Chapter Five

Marriage

At some point in early adulthood, many men get married and can rarely verbalize the reasons why they did so. Reasons for getting married barely get considered except by the insightful, the frightened, or those who are reluctant to settle down. Once men get married, a big adjustment is in order. Although couples overtly struggle over money, sex and kids, the underlying issues are power and intimacy. Throughout the search for a partner and the attempt to make a marriage work, the subtle fears of loss of power and the sadness of not meeting one's need for intimacy pervade men's struggle to form a marital union.

Readiness

What makes one man ready to get married while others avoid it? I believe that it has to do with the amount of responsibility and commitment that he's ready to assume, and his awareness of his need for intimacy. It's these two parts of a man's life that must come together in order for a man to be ready for marriage and have a chance at success. Some men don't marry, which has been examined in detail by Charles Waehler in his book, *Bachelors: The psychology of men who haven't married*. I will focus here on those men who do marry or establish a committed relationship.

One factor that motivates a man to marry is that he feels that he's completed what he thinks he's supposed to have completed in his career. In other words, when he feels powerful enough at work then he can take the chance to meet his need for intimacy.

This feeling of well-being about his career progress is a clue that tells him that he's ready to take on the next task of adulthood; i.e., marriage. With career security and/or prospects for future success intact, he's ready to nest.

Dan, a successful attorney, described his readiness as, ."..something that I knew was more than a desire for sex or for a steady date. I guess that I would have gotten married sooner, but I haven't had time to date much because I've been working so many hours, and I've been pretty tired. My focus has been on getting my career on track."

Scott reported a different point by saying, "I looked around at my friends who got married, fixed up an apartment and were making a future together. I thought that I could do that too. I dated Marie for a long time. I know her very well, and she knows me. I've done well at my job, and I think that we'll do okay as a married couple."

A second factor motivating men toward marriage is that a man has experienced a feeling of isolation, similar to loneliness. Awareness of this feeling leads him to conclude that intimacy can be gained only through a committed relationship.

Jeff made a very honest and perceptive self-analysis when he remarked, "My interest in getting married started when I admitted that I just didn't like living alone. I felt that way even when I was living in my parents' house, but I wouldn't admit it to myself back then."

When considering marriage, men would be wise to evaluate what I consider to be the single most important personality factor in determining the success or failure of marital relationships -- independence. Men who examine this factor carefully might make a better choice of a partner than men who don't.

Independence

Independence is defined by many men as feeling in control of their own behavior without the influence of someone else. When men talk about feeling independent, they usually mean feeling powerful. Their motivation to be independent may also be based upon a fear of losing power. Specifically, a highly independent man may fear that the people on whom he depends (or might depend) will fail him. He may believe that to be truly powerful he must be free from reliance upon others. Of course, every man has some fear of getting hurt, but extreme independence can mean that men distance themselves so far from others that they isolate themselves.

Scott, a self-proclaimed independent man, age twenty-nine and separated from his wife, described himself to be "...able to relate to others or not, depending on what I want to do. I'm not going to wait for others to decide on what I'm going to do either socially or at work. I want to stand or fall on what I do. With women, I'm interested, attentive and generous. I know that I don't want someone to take care of me, but I don't mind taking care of others." After a bit of probing, he said, "I guess that I'm a little afraid of relying on others instead of myself. My father always said that if you wanted something done right you should do it yourself. I guess I've applied that philosophy to relationships."

At the other extreme, a man who fears that he might fail the people who rely on him is vulnerable to become highly dependent. To avoid failure he'll depend on others instead of letting people depend on him. He believes that he cannot be powerful enough to care for others effectively, and so he relies on the power of others instead of trying to be powerful on his own. Excessive dependence, like excessive independence, does not make men function well in marriage.

Dan, the attorney, who is on the dependent side of the scale, said, "I like to have resources around me, like my friends. I feel comfortable with others who understand and accept me. People, who are needy and clinging, like some women I've dated, make me uncomfortable. I guess I don't want to take care of someone else. I sometimes say that I need most of my time and energy to take care of myself. You know, like taking care of others wasn't a good thing to do. I think that I was afraid of rescuing people who should take care of themselves and was confusing them with people who had ordinary needs for comfort and companionship."

As a general guideline, an independent man should choose someone who will not want him to rely on her too much for intellectual consultation or emotional support. Perhaps a woman on the dependent side would be a good choice for this man.

Conversely, the dependent man should avoid a woman who wants a person on whom she can lean and by whom she can by guided. An independent woman would be a wise selection for this man. Of course, most men must make some adjustments after marriage that allow their need for power to be fulfilled while meeting the needs of their spouse.

Adjustment after Marriage

The adjustment required by marriage is the biggest and most difficult adjustment that men ever have to face, regardless of what age they marry. Newly-married men often feel a sense of "diminished competence" because they must share power with their spouse (except in very traditional marriages where the husband does not share). Many men find shared power (which is less power than they had when they were single) to be very uncomfortable. In addition, men must cope with a spouse who is trying to meet her own needs.

The issues most frequently reported by divorcing couples in early adulthood as being the cause of their breakup are money, sex and children (if any). Actually, these issues are the surface manifestations of the underlying conflict of sharing power and meeting intimacy needs, in my opinion.

Money

In many cases a husband experiences "diminished competence" because he believes that there's not enough money to have the goods and services that he or his wife want. Either he blames himself for not making enough income (thus feeling powerless to make enough money) or else he blames his wife's spending habits (thus feeling powerless to meet her needs or to make her stop spending). No matter whom he blames, he feels less powerful than before he got married. As he feels less powerful, he will either withdraw in depressed silence from intimate contact with his wife or else he'll fight with her, which also diminishes the intimacy between them.

A struggling young husband said, "We never seem to get ahead, and we don't have very much. I like working at XYZ, but I feel bad a lot when I think about what I can provide for Janet and me. She tries to reassure me, but I think underneath that she's disappointed in me."

Take the case of Tim, age twenty-seven and employed as an electrician. He and his wife, who both work in secure occupations, have a mid-level income, two kids, and no big financial burdens except for a mortgage. She reported, "We have terrible fights over sneakers for the kids, an extra blouse for our daughter, or a shirt for our son. Any purchase seen by Tim as the least bit unnecessary starts an argument. It's been going on like this for years."

At first Tim resisted his wife's accusation that he was tight with money by rationalizing her concerns. He said, "You don't realize that we need money for the future and for a rainy day." Of course, the real issue was how scared Tim was of letting go of some control of his family. Many therapy sessions later, Tim admitted, "Yes, I am scared of what could happen. I'd never forgive myself if I couldn't live up to what I expect of myself as a husband. Maybe by trying so hard to be a provider I do come on too strong."

Many men use economic control of family funds as a way of wielding power. It's a destructive tactic, but insecurity leads men to act in ways that alienate their wives.

Sex

A typical complaint of a husband in early adulthood is that he and his wife don't have sex frequently enough. Not having something when he wants it means that he isn't as powerful as he'd like to be (or thinks he should be). The problem is compounded by the memory of when he was first dating, was first married, and had sex more often. Sometimes the frequency rate of intercourse goes from seven times a week at the time of marriage to once a week within six months to a year. Most couples married more than two years, who are in their late twenties and are both employed or have at least one child, have sex once a week on Saturday night between the hours of ten o'clock and midnight. These statistics are rarely comforting to men.

Again Tim said, "I know that I'd like to have sex more often, but Bonnie's just not interested. Maybe I'm losing my touch or something. She's not as excited by me as when we were first married, but I don't know why."

Men contribute to the infrequent sex issue by confusing physical and emotional intimacy. Most men want to be intimate but use the physical or action orientation instead of the verbal method. It doesn't mean that men are insensitive, just uninformed and misguided. Tim reported, "Bonnie and I are kind of apart over sex right now. I like the feeling of closeness that I get when she and I have sex, but she accuses me of not being sensitive to her feelings and needs. I think she means that I don't listen to her enough and let her talk without giving my opinion about what she should do. I also don't think she gives me enough credit for the things I do around the apartment in order to show her that I'm concerned about her. She says that I either try to please her or I try to protect her. I don't know what's so wrong with that."

In addition, women want physical contact such as hugs and touches that do not lead to sexual advances. Physical contact without sexual feelings is very difficult for many men. The more trouble they have with having non-sexual physical contact in general, the less intimacy they will experience.

Tim continued by saying, "Bonnie used to sit next to me on the sofa, but now she reads in the bedroom or in another part of the living room. She says that I either ignore her because I'm watching television or I try to fondle her and make a sexual pass at her. I don't know what to do."

With practice and understanding, men can become more verbally expressive, and women can become more accepting of men's acting-out method of communication. Intimacy can be communicated non-verbally, but must be differentiated from sexually-motivated contacts.

A second concern of many men is that they believe that they typically initiate sex and would like their wives to approach them more often. Being approached sexually means to most men that they are attractive, and they gain great satisfaction from this knowledge. Some other men like being approached because they want to feel that they have the upper hand, if only for a moment perhaps, when they have the power to accept or deny their wives's request.

A frustrated husband complained, "I'm always affectionate toward Barb, but she's never approached me to have sex. I'm always the one who wants to. Like she's some kind of reluctant princess or something. I really would like to know that she wants to have sex with me instead of just going along with my suggestion."

An extreme sexual problem for men is sexual dysfunction such as impotence. In some marriages this problem leads to divorce. Usually men feel ashamed because they accept all of the blame for the problem, but some men blame their wives and want to escape. A sexual dysfunction problem almost always, in my opinion, starts in the marital relationship and is not the problem itself.

Sexual dysfunction occurs in a relationship, I believe, in which a man feels a sense of diminished power, which leads to depression or anger. The powerlessness can come from work or from a sense that he has disappointed his wife at home. A sensitive man takes the real or imagined disappointment of his wife to heart, sometimes unconsciously. The anger can come from a feeling of being criticized by his wife for disappointing her. Internalized anger has a terrible effect on men, even without their knowing that they're angry.

After a few sessions of psychotherapy, Randy, a man with an impotence problem, said, "Yes, I guess I am angry at Phyllis for her criticism of me. But I never thought I was so angry with her that I couldn't have sex. I always thought that my sexual problem was all my fault. You know, I was just tired or something. After I was able to have sex with my old girl friend, I know that my problem's just with Phyllis and not with all women. I'm not proud of what I did with my old girlfriend, but I am relieved. I hope that Phyllis and I can work things out. I'm ready for us both to meet with you."

After a few months of therapy, Tim and Bonnie had removed some of the barriers to their intimacy and had resumed a more satisfying sexual relationship. Tim stated, "It's hard for me to understand that Bonnie doesn't want me to take care of her and protect her in the ways that I thought were good to do. But I can accept that she wants to be valued as a competent and self-sufficient person who can make it on her own two feet. That still scares me, but I'll handle it. It's sure a different way of thinking about a marriage. At least for me it is."

Children

The birth of a child changes everything. A man goes from being responsible for himself to being responsible for a wife and then for a child as well. The change from single to married is tough enough, but at least in marriage a man is dealing with a rational person with whom he's spent several months or years getting to know. For most couples, preparing for a baby only means picking out names and baby furniture. It's impossible to imagine during this blissful period of anticipation how much a baby will disrupt their relationship.

A frequent subject of conflict is how to raise the kids. A key issue is discipline. For instance, the wife wants to punish by taking away a toy and the husband by spanking. Or, the wife wants the child to be punished for misbehavior and the husband feels it should be ignored. It always becomes a conflict of power. When the husband wants to feel in control of the child and his wife disagrees, he feels frustrated and criticized. If, on the other hand, he wants his wife to discipline the child and she asks for his help, he may feel fearful of making an error in how to discipline.

Larry and Sue illustrate an example of a common type of power struggle. Larry, the twenty-eight year old hospital administrator under a lot of pressure at work, confided, "Sue is very lax about rules. I'm stricter about schedules, and that's what I think is best for our daughter no matter how old she is. If she's on a schedule of eating and sleeping and playing, then she'll be happier than if she's not. Also Sue and I will be able to have more time together. I just can't get Sue to be more disciplined."

In addition, a husband and wife may disagree over how much to be involved with the kids. A typical pattern is the overinvolved wife and the underinvolved husband. She does all or most of the childcare, and he does little other than play with the kids or help at bedtime occasionally. Often this happens because the husband feels truly incompetent at childraising and avoids these activities as much as possible. Other times men feel demeaned by child-raising tasks, which they see as mundane and unimportant and, consequently, they avoid them. Many women tire of this inequity quickly. Resentment begins, and resentment leads to conflict.

Scott told me, "I always thought that Marie knew more than I did about babies and children, so I let her do all the stuff that needs to be done. I'm willing to help her in any way she asks me to. I guess I don't jump in to help as much as I could. It's kind of hard for me to play with an infant, though. It's not like we can have a conversation."

Sometimes resentment results in violence. Violence is often reported as "the problem", but it's actually a symptom, a terrible symptom, of power needs going unmet in a relationship where there's not enough intimacy to give voice to the problems. Sometimes the hostility is turned inward and the result is alcohol or drug abuse, or even suicide.

A man who has trouble sharing power with his wife in the rearing of children must overcome the fear that he'll lose his position of protector and provider. Men who do not feel a loss of power when a child arrives may experience a sense of diminished intimacy, which can be just as damaging as the feeling of decreased power.

All of a sudden someone has come between the man and his wife, and he's supposed to make space for this new person's intrusion. Suddenly, it's hard to have a conversation, let alone sex.

Time alone with each other has diminished dramatically, and there is little time for friendships with others. Lots of confusing feelings toward the baby begin to affect the marital relationship.

Many men feel this loss of intimacy and demand more time and attention. At the same time, the baby's needs mean the wife is less available. The common result that I have seen is that the man feels abandoned and rejected.

Again, Larry confided, "I hate to admit how hurt I've been. I don't want to blame the baby. And I don't want to blame Sue either. I guess that we've got a problem together, like you told us. It's solvable, but not in the ways I've been trying. We've got to reach a compromise."

After a big fight with Marie during which she demanded that Scott stop being so passive and uninvolved with her and the baby, Scott was shocked. He said to me, "I can't believe that Marie was so upset and angry with me. I was scared of doing the wrong thing before, and now I'm scared to not do something. I guess anything that I volunteer to do with the baby is okay with Marie." I challenged his earlier reason for avoiding childcare, which was his lack of skill compared to Marie's skill level.

He admitted, "I really wanted us to have the same relationship that we had before the baby came. You know, lots of walks and being alone together. I suppose that I thought that we could still do that if she could take care of the baby herself. I know now that I was resisting the baby entering our lives."

In addition to wanting more time and attention, most men think: "I want to think of my wife as an attractive woman, not someone like my mom"; and "I want to think of myself as a young, attractive, fun guy, not as an old, unattractive, boring father." In other words they want: a woman, not a mother, who is a woman as young as themselves.

A woman not a mother

Men want to have a sexually attractive wife. After the birth of a child, a wife becomes a mother. For some men, this means she can no longer be sexy or fun-loving. It's the image men have of mothers as saints or as dumpy women in aprons. Many men learned this cultural myth as children, and they exaggerated it out of proportion when they became adults. Men who continue to hold this belief, and many do without knowing it, pull away from their wives socially and sexually. In so doing, they give up their primary source of intimacy.

A woman as young as myself

Some men want a wife to keep them young. The woman they married cannot, somehow, be young and a mother at the same time. In the minds of these men, mothers are old. Because these men are married to a mother, that makes them old too. Consequently, many men feel depressed after the birth of a child. These men believe that only the young are powerful or have the chance to be powerful. Unfortunately, these men often blame their wives for their unidentified distress, which they express either by fighting or withdrawal.

On the positive side, some men feel older after the birth of a child, which helps them feel more responsible. They realize they'll always be a father to their children, and finally they're a complete adult in the eyes of society. The increased responsibility, another step toward full adulthood, and the sense of being older are a reward for some men and a burden for others.

The reward comes from the powerful feeling embodied by the declaration: "Now, I am a man." To many men, it's the ultimate validation of manhood.

The burden, of course, is that there's now a person who will depend on this man for the rest of his life. At first, it will be physical dependence and later emotional dependence. Even men who first experience fatherhood as a reward may later feel its burden. At one extreme is a father who perceives his child as a direct extension of himself. He may feel so overwhelmed by the responsibility that he'll try to be the sole influence in the child's life, and so will become overprotective and authoritarian. At the other extreme is a father who abandons his responsibility (usually to the child's mother) rather than make a mistake.

How a father reacts to the role will shape his relationship with his child for the rest of their lives. One man will accept the reward and think of fatherhood as a challenge. He'll plunge ahead with the confidence that somehow he and his child will flourish no matter what happens. A different man will proceed with cautious detachment.

Some men are not ready to accept the responsibility of marriage and fatherhood and the test of power that a marriage and children imply. Others are ready but can't make the adjustment that marriage and fatherhood require. Some men select a mate without adequately assessing how their respective needs for independence and dependence will mesh. When hope that the marriage will improve is gone, divorce seems to be the only answer.

Divorce

Ending a marriage causes a shock that is almost as profound as marriage and fatherhood and certainly is more painful. Every man knows about divorce, but no one thinks that it will happen to him.

One man on the brink of divorce said, "I never thought about divorce before I got married. My parents never got divorced and neither did my aunts and uncles. When Melissa and I got married, everything was going great. At least I thought so. We gradually stopped talking, and she was moody all the time. I know that I was busy, but so was she. We liked our jobs, and were doing well there. She just seemed dissatisfied at home all the time. Nothing I could do would please her. Maybe I didn't pay enough attention to her. I know that I can get wrapped up in work and other things, like sports on TV."

A second man reported, "Patty and I disagree about a lot of things, like money, having kids, our parents, where to live, who to associate with. I want to wait to have kids, and to save money, but she wants everything right away. I avoid talking about anything, I guess. Divorce seems to be the only way to get out of arguing all the time. I always feel under pressure to make more or do more or do something better than I'm already doing. I sometimes think that our daughter is just another thing that Patty wants. All we do is argue about her, too."

A third man stated, "We never disagreed about stuff at first, but now we do. It seems that we never know how to please the other person. We don't have fights; I almost wish we would. I hate conflict, and so maybe we just avoid each other. We treat each other with respect but never get to know how to deal with each other except as roommates. It's easy to be attracted to other people who seem more open."

Most divorced men feel defeated. Feeling defeated or like a failure is typical among men who look upon marriage as an accomplishment. If they have a good marriage then they're proving to the world and to themselves that they are competent and successful, which is a reflection of their power.

After his divorce one man told me he felt, "Really down. And I don't know what I could have done differently. I've failed somehow, and I feel terrible. If I can't make it work with Pam, then I don't know if I can make it with someone else."

Some men feel guilty for not trying hard enough. This may or may not be true and can never be proved, of course, so men are left with an unending doubt.

The divorced man with children may feel defeated and guilty not only because the marriage ended but also because he can't be a fully-functioning father. A divorced father told me, "Having a child you can't see when you want to is rough. I think that I would have made a good father if the marriage had worked out. (Pause) I'll never get the chance now."

A resentful father said he felt, "cheated." He said angrily, "I have the right to know my daughter just as well as her mother knows her, but that can't happen because I don't have custody. Maybe it's better if I just drop out of the picture completely."

In a soft voice, one man simply told me, "I didn't get a chance to be a father because I was having so much trouble being a husband." It's not easy to handle the loss of a spouse and a child too.

Some men avoid their children to avoid the pain of a failed marriage. A man who was divorced for eight years began seeing his son regularly after visiting him previously only once or twice a year. When asked about it, he said, "I guess I'm feeling better about myself. I'm able to accept what I did to cause the breakup with Marlene. I want to accept my son as one of the good parts of my marriage. I want to keep that part. I can do that now without feeling so badly about the divorce."

Men who marry and remain married through early adulthood and men who divorce during this time probably reach middle adulthood at different times. Married men usually expand their lives to take on more responsibility. Divorced men seem either to begin the search for a mate again, throw themselves into their work to avoid the pain, or retreat from life's challenges temporarily. Middle adulthood provides chances for additional power and intimacy for both groups of men.

Chapter Six

The Beginning of Middle Adulthood

The Plan

The man entering middle adulthood, usually in his thirties, although perhaps older, has laid the groundwork for a lifestyle that will last for his middle adulthood years and perhaps for the rest of his life. The foundation of this lifestyle is the balance between meeting his need for power and meeting his need for intimacy. Although he may have established this balance intuitively; nevertheless, he has developed some plan for his life and some method or process for achieving that plan.

The implementation of a plan forged during early adulthood dominates the decades of the thirties, forties, fifties and beyond. However, around thirty, a man may have reviewed his strategy for life and made some changes. The man who asked himself "Did I make the right decision about a career, a mate, children, and friends?" has answered this question by now and has taken appropriate action either to change or to stay the course forged by earlier experiences.

The man who said "Yes" to the question about his decisions will forge ahead to try to carry out the next set of tasks that society has set forth. These tasks could include having a second child, accepting a position of more social recognition, seeking more financial security, or increasing involvement in social events among friends or in church or civic groups.

The man who answered "No" to the question about his decisions will take one of two possible actions. One action is to "correct" his decisions by getting a new job, a divorce or by making some other major change that will alter the direction of his life in the coming decades. A man told me, "I married Ellen when I was eighteen and only now, at thirty, I understand the reasons. My mother died when I was thirteen, and my father's drinking got worse. It got to the point that he was drunk and abusive most of the time. I wanted to escape, and I guess I did. It made sense at the time, I guess. But that's not a reason for me to stay married to her. I guess I made a mistake."

Men must realize that they didn't know enough about themselves or about other people during early adulthood, so that they were quite likely to make a "mistake." The important thing is to learn from these "mistakes" and make the changes that they deem necessary.

Another action that a man at the transition to middle adulthood could take is to decide that such major shifts are too much to handle. In doing so, he accepts the direction that his choices of the twenties take him, however bad these choices may seem to be. He may admit that he made a "mistake", but then decide that he can live with the consequences. This may mean that he must endure a job that is dissatisfying. It may mean that he must put up with a marriage that is unfulfilling. For most men, accepting their plan feels like they have "settled" for less than they deserve and that feels bad. Let's take a brief look at some men who "settle."

A man who "settles" for a less than satisfying life situation, whatever it may be, does so for one of several reasons. One reason is that he has other areas in his life that are so satisfying that they compensate for the dissatisfying area in which he's chosen to "settle." The man with a disappointing marriage might pour energy into his work. The man with a meaningless job could coach youth sports. Some compensation is necessary for survival because men can't start over each time they hit a dead end. Of course, no compensatory activity is completely satisfying, and not every man has areas into which he can shift his time and energy in order to get more satisfaction.

Another reason why a man "settles" is that he fears the pain that making a change would bring in the short run, despite his belief that making the change would work out well in the long run. A man, who thought about divorcing his wife said, "I know that it would be better for me, eventually, and for Diane too, but I know how disappointed I would be in myself. I just can't bring myself to face that."

Avoidance of anticipated pain doesn't engender any deeply felt satisfaction but when a man thinks about why he "settled", he can gain only a sense of relief. The absence of pain does not equal happiness, but instead equals a numbness, which some men find to be better than suffering.

The way a man implements his plan in the beginning of middle adulthood is as important as the plan itself. Some men work as fast as they can and others move slowly. The high-energy man works hard to make things happen. He may be easily disappointed and may be anxious and upset when the plan doesn't work out. He's intense and probably seems frustrated at times. The slow moving man is calm and easy-going and also believes that he's not (and never was) totally in control of his life events. He's analytic and introspective about himself and others and knows how to laugh at himself. Let's look at examples of each of these processes.

The Process

Bill and Larry

Bill is an attorney in a large firm and wants to become a partner in order to gain financial security, a larger salary, and recognition of his competence. His wife, Linda, is a high school guidance counselor and works full time. They have two daughters, ages eight and four. Although Bill feels confident about his work, he knows that he could do better by being more thoroughly prepared. He is often intimidated by senior people in the firm who have knowledge that surpasses his own and a casual way of expressing it. He avoids these people.

Socially, Bill plays racquetball once a week with a colleague from his office and goes out to dinner with this colleague and his wife and Linda. The conversation at these dinners is usually work-related. Bill has no hobbies or other people with whom he socializes, although he speaks to his parents weekly on the phone. His parents and Linda's parents live nearby and often visit Bill and Linda. Bill and Linda rarely travel to their parents' home for visits.

Bill says, "I like what I do, and I'm good at it. I don't feel very recognized by others for my achievements or my efforts though. Everyone in the firm is very competent and hard-working, and they all want to be partners. Not everyone will make it. I know that I focus a lot on work and that Linda and I don't do much together or with the kids, but it will be better in a few years after I make partner and can relax."

He continues about his fantasy for himself. "I guess I want to be successful. I suppose that means to make a secure financial environment for my family and myself and to have security in my job. If I really work during my thirties I'll have a secure position for the rest of my life."

A similar man is Larry, who works as the number two person in the marketing division of a large company that manufactures and distributes soap throughout the country. Larry is married to Sarah who works full-time as a computer programmer for a local company. They have no children. Larry believes that his future looks good if he continues to do the traveling (eight to ten days per month) and the back-up work for his boss who may become senior vice-president and one day president. He finds himself with too little time at the office to do his work because of his travel schedule. Although he's been promoted rapidly and given salary increases, he's not sure of his future at all.

Socially, Larry spends his time entertaining clients or out-of-town colleagues who visit the home office for meetings. Sarah rarely accompanies him on these occasions because other men's wives rarely travel with them. Sarah plans a social schedule for the two of them, which ranges from movies, plays, and concerts to dinner with neighbors and friends of hers from her job. She also plans for regular (every several months) visits to see Larry's parents who live about two hours away. Sarah's parents live out of state. Larry plays tennis almost weekly with a colleague. Recently, he's become unhappy with his partner, as his game is not improving. Additionally, he jogs and has begun to enter local 5 and 10 kilometer races. He has begun to "train", rather than merely jog for exercise.

Larry says, "I work hard to get to the point where I'm going to be in a position that won't get dumped in any reorganization. I'm liked by my boss, who's moving up rapidly, and will keep me with him. If he leaves, it will be a different story. Several years ago I thought about leaving and doing something else, probably in sales, which I really like. It would have meant moving, but Sarah was very resistant to leaving her job and friends. Sarah and I get along very well. She helps me to relax and loosen up a little."

When asked about his fantasy of middle adulthood or life plan, Larry said quite readily, "I'd like to be on my own; doing what I want to do, not following the directions of others all the time. I used to think that I wanted to be in charge of other people and have them carry out my ideas and directions. I direct people now, but the ideas and directions are handed down from someone higher up. I'd like to be on my own, or with one or two others, in a small company."

Several themes emerge from the discussions with Bill and Larry. The first theme is that they are concerned about financial security for themselves and their family. Perhaps these men are trying to make enough money so that they can buy anything that will make them feel better and never have to say "no" to a child's request for a toy or an Ivy League education. These men, and others like them, have some concern for the future during early adulthood, but the concern accelerates in middle adulthood. It's difficult to challenge a man who says he's concerned about his kids because of the high cost of raising a child. And who isn't motivated to work hard when they see the rate at which businesses fail? A future orientation and a desire to make the future financially stable are fine but may be a delusion if these men believe that power guarantees security.

A second theme for Larry and Bill is that they have few friendships and spend little time in social activities in which true friendships might develop. Acquaintances may be formed, but that's all. Social occasions often become an extension of work. Relaxing isn't as easy as it would appear to be, even a week's vacation. A woman analyzed, "For the first two days of our week at the shore, Gary is very irritable and tries to get the kids and me on some sort of schedule to play tennis or swim or ride bikes. He's eager to do everything, but is agitated. Then he slows down and is depressed for two days. He withdraws from us and reads or walks by himself mostly. I think he misses work, or the challenge of work, or the routine of it. Finally, he rejoins us and is fun to be with. He lets others set the pace, doesn't try to do everything, and handles disruptions, like bad weather, with no fuss."

Another theme for men like Larry and Bill is their recreation pattern. Such men turn leisure-time activities into work. The tennis player who works on his backhand against a wall, the jogger who measures his distance and times himself, and the basement craftsman who sells his works all have added another "career" to their list instead of shifting their focus from career to leisure activity. When men change from exercising as leisure to exercise as vocation, they talk about "training" or being "in training" for an upcoming event, match, race, or contest.

One sidelight is that these men work at a damaging pace. Many of them put in a long day or two (or a week), go on a sales trip, or have a busy season and then have a slow period. This change in intensity is very tough on men, I believe. The more frequent the changes, the more damage they sustain. In my opinion a sudden and frequent change in pace causes burnout more often than a consistently rapid pace or one of consistently high intensity.

A fourth theme of these men, illustrated by Larry and Bill, is the wish for autonomy in a career. These men desire the freedom to create, implement, or manage their work activities with less direction, control, or evaluation by others in authority. These middle adulthood men yearn to test their abilities without restraint. They feel stifled and want to leave the security of the organization that protects them.

One last theme that describes men with this pattern is that their family provides a respite or escape from work, but little intimacy. These men rest with family and gain strength for the next burst of energy that will be needed at work, but gain little nurturance and satisfaction. There are two different theories or cultural myths to explain this situation.

One theory, or commonly accepted myth, is that men who recharge at home are worn out from work and so they don't have much to give at home. Accepting this theory justifies men's withdrawal from family and friends into passive and solitary forms of relaxation. According to this theory a man is like an automobile battery that has a maximum charge against which the automobile takes what is needed. Periodic recharges can never push the battery past a pre-determined level. These men withhold at home because they don't think that they'll have enough to give at work if they give too much at home. Their need for power is so strong that they focus their attention on the area where they want to prove themselves most. If this is an accurate description of the male identity, then the man who expends all of his energy at work deserves no blame for giving little or nothing at home. His wife and kids can be mad at him, but he believes (and tries to convince them) that he has nothing left to give. Some men will even get their wives and kids to feel sympathy for them, for a while at least. It's the fault of the job and not the man, the theory states.

A second theory or belief is that men have "unlimited energy." In this theory men have a reserve tank that takes over when they're out of energy from their usual supply. They rarely use this tank because they fear that when they get low on energy that the reserve tank won't function. If this is an accurate explanation of male development, then men are completely responsible for their behavior. There's no acceptable excuse for avoiding their family. If a man doesn't give at home then it's because he doesn't want to give there. In this view, the man is responsible and not the job.

I believe in the "unlimited energy" theory that men have an unlimited source of energy, and they can tap it whenever they want to do so. There's even one step further.

Spending time with family or friends and being intimate with them creates energy in my view. Helping with chores or homework can create energy. Energy can be gained by phoning a friend, doing an errand with a child, playing a game or helping with a decision. The idea is that creating energy is done through intimate interactions with others. It's not the activity itself but the intimate contact that is important.

Jeff and Ken

Jeff has a college degree in business and reviews documents and forms in a large office of the federal government. He's married to Susan who works at home by caring for their two children. Jeff believes that his work is important and that he's good at it, although he'd like to have more responsibility. Socially, he works with youth athletic teams, including baseball and soccer, and is active in his church as the chairman of a major committee. Jeff, Susan, and their children visit both his parents and Susan's parents regularly and keep frequent contact with their siblings who all live in the nearby area. They spend much of their leisure time in family activities such as trips to the zoo or picnics and spend little time with neighbors and friends. Jeff exercises only in the course of doing home repairs or playing with the kids.

Jeff says, "I like my job alright. I could do more if I had the chance. I know that I can move up if I get more education and training, but I'm not worried about being pushed out of my present job by somebody else. I like my family and enjoy my activities with them."

When asked about a fantasy or life plan, Jeff replied, "My fantasy was to be a professional athlete or else an artist. I never had the athletic ability to go pro, but I played all through college even though I was aware that I didn't have the ability to go any further. As an artist I have some talent, but I didn't want to struggle in poverty for years and maybe never be successful enough to support a family. I enjoy going to museums and art shows and helping my kids develop their artistic talents."

Another example of a man who has accepted his choices of early adulthood is Ken, an auto mechanic for a large truck rental company. He's successful at work but is often bored with the routine nature of the tasks he performs. He feels adequately rewarded both financially and personally by his boss. Ken is secure about his future with the company and his ability to go somewhere else should that become necessary. He'd like to do more trouble-shooting of the difficult jobs. He's also taking a college course (his first) at night in business administration. Ken's married to Laura and they have three children. Laura works part-time as a secretary/typist for a realtor. Ken socializes with two men friends from work by playing cards or bowling one night each week in a league. He and Laura spend time on weekends socializing with neighbors playing cards at each other's homes or attending a football game or hockey game. They see their parents about once every month.

Ken says, "I like my job and feel confident about what's expected of me. I would like to see what it's like to manage the whole shop, do estimates, set up the work schedule, and all. I feel secure about the future. I enjoy what I do outside of work, just taking it easy with the guys I hang around with and our neighbors."

About a fantasy or plan, Ken replied, "I really never had any long-term fantasy other than I wanted to do something mechanical, which I enjoy, and to be happy. I never thought about making a lot of money or of having a lot of things. I've thought about opening my own shop, but I know I wouldn't want the headaches that a small business owner has. I do worry sometimes if I've been successful enough for Laura. She's got more training than I do, and she works around educated people all day."

The first pattern for men like Jeff and Ken is that they have jobs in fields that offer a high degree of security. The security of a steady job and a regular raise in salary allows them to feel confident about the future. Job security offers validation to men who need to know that their sense of power may never be challenged. If these men never have to change jobs then they never will be faced with the feelings of failure and powerlessness that occur when seeking a new position. Security needs are more important than needs for challenge and autonomy for these men. However, if a man has had a dream that he never acted on, and he's at a point in life where he has less of an economic burden on him (grown children, a working wife) then he may seek a change. This change is often called a mid-life crisis and is usually judged to be negative, but it doesn't have to be.

A middle adulthood man who wants to change his career in order to take a chance at a dream he wanted a decade earlier should usually take the risk, in my opinion. Stress, economic hardship, and ridicule from friends and family may accompany a career change, but the attempt is worth the effort, in my opinion. I believe that it's better for a man to have tried and failed than to stay in a secure job feeling bitter and disappointed that he never tried to reach his dream.

A second theme for Jeff and Ken and others like them is that they are more involved in areas outside their work than men like Bill and Larry. They have security from their work and look for affiliation and a feeling of competence from social, recreational, family, and civic or religious life. Jeff and Ken have a more equal balance between the power and intimacy they receive than Larry and Bill. This balance is likely to lead them to be more satisfied with life than Larry and Bill, who are more interested in achieving power than intimacy.

New Challenges at Work

In middle adulthood men use the information they have gained through the experimentation of early adulthood. They use this information to attain greater achievement and advancement. Furthermore, the dream of themselves as workers has become more realistic in terms of choosing an appropriate field. How much they can achieve has yet to be discovered. At this stage of adulthood men strive for the security that they believe will come from having enough power. In other words, to feel powerful is to feel that one has a sense of control over day-to-day events as well as the general course of one's life.

The belief that power can bring about security is deeply ingrained in American society, but unfortunately, I believe, it's not true for most men. Consider the payoff for the man who is very future-oriented and uses power to gain as many material goods as possible during middle adulthood in order to retire early or to ensure that his financial future will be secure for the next several decades. This intense concentration on the future is often motivated by a need to protect himself from the possibility of having to rely on others for his financial or physical care later in life. It shows an insecurity that says "I can't really trust in my family or friends to help me if I need money." It could also be saying, "I can't trust my own ability to provide for myself and my family, and so I have to work hard now when I have the energy and the opportunity. I may not have either in the coming decades."

This pattern of "push yourself now so you can relax later" is usually ineffective and destructive, in my opinion. The hard-driving man is unlikely to be able to suddenly sit back and feel that he has enough financial security. A setback could happen at any time. I believe that he will always feel vulnerable about losing the wealth that he's gained. It's as if the more a man has, the more he has to lose. The emotional cost to a man who attempts to calm his insecurity through the accumulation of goods and/or influence is a large one. This man gives up his social and family life, thus sacrificing his opportunity for intimacy. A single-minded search for power guarantees loneliness. This man misses out on the warmth of friendship and the joy of spontaneous moments. He also eliminates resources on whom he can call in times of stress.

So the answer to the question, "Can power bring about security?" is "No." All men need to feel powerful, but the struggle to gain enough of it to feel secure often results in feeling disappointed or frustrated. Disappointment can lead to depression. Frustration can be expressed as rage.

When the Need for Power Goes Unmet

The need for power can be in direct conflict with the need for security, even though many men try to gain security through the achievement of power. In order to advance and achieve, one must take risks. If a man wants too much security then he is less likely to take the risks needed to move ahead.

In addition, the responsibilities of middle adulthood men, such as a wife (or ex-wife), children, and debts prompt many men to take fewer risks and so lessen their chances for career advancement. They see the conflict as "I can't change jobs to get greater prestige, because I'll lower our standard of living" or "If I go out on my own, I might not make it financially, and that would hurt my family. I don't mind the hardship for myself but not for my wife and kids."

Middle adulthood men handle this dilemma in one of several ways. The most typical pattern men follow, in my view, is to deny their need for power and take the safest path to economic security and family stability. They say, "I've got to accept my responsibilities to others first. Then I can meet my own needs if possible." This sounds reasonable, but there's a problem. The sacrifice that men make to gain security often is too great. If the need for power is not met sufficiently, problems will arise of a magnitude that will be damaging both physically and interpersonally. Here's a further explanation.

The man who chooses to stay at his job with few opportunities for gaining economic rewards or interpersonal influence may become increasingly depressed at his powerlessness. It will be seen in his withdrawal from social activities, disturbed sleep, lack of appetite, and lack of interest in sex. He may seek relief by excessive use of alcohol or other drugs.

A second pattern of men's reacting to an unmet need for power at work is to seek power in areas other than work. Some men will try to be more powerful by involvement in a union or in a professional organization. Others might seek satisfaction through power in a social group or community activity. Men often find these substitutes to be very beneficial and are termed compensating activities.

Compensating activities, in my view, can be good or bad. Good activities are those that help a man feel powerful without hurting others or establishing a life-style that is out of balance. Take the marathon runner, the karate black belt, the local politician, the model airplane builder, or the charity fund-raiser who works just as hard on his avocation as on his vocation or maybe even harder. These men have found that with a little effort they can feel more powerful than they have felt in their careers. In contrast to their job, they can accomplish a goal be it physical (exercise, athletics), mental (higher education, chess), or interpersonal (politics, civic work). Some men find compensating activities so rewarding that they get carried away and overcompensate. This is when compensating activities can be bad. Men spend so much time in this compensatory activity that other aspects of their lives suffer. It's usually a man's interpersonal relations with family and friends that become neglected.

A third pattern of response to an unmet need for power is to escape the ties of responsibility that bind them by divorce or abandonment. It's a desperate attempt for men to feel good about themselves. Escape only works temporarily as a method of dealing with unmet needs in my observation. Eventually, men seem to feel guilty about having escaped, and this guilt is painful. Men must find some other place to meet their need for power if they can't satisfy it at work.

An example of escapes are those activities which blot out the disappointment of unmet power needs such as drugs, alcohol, gambling or an extra-marital affair. Of course, men have affairs for a variety of reasons, but I believe that they often have an affair if they feel a lack of power in their work and in interpersonal relations with others, including their wives. The excitement of sex and romance allows them to escape the feelings of powerlessness. An affair with an attractive woman says to a man that he has influence over another person. He feels especially powerful because this woman cares for him even though he's married to someone else and is not eligible.

Gaining power often pushes a man away from the intimacy that other people offer him. In American culture, being powerful means being strong and defended. However, being strong and defended prevents the intimate affiliation that is so important for maintenance and growth of mental health.

Man the Machine

The difficulty in climbing the ladder of success is that men learn to deal with the frustrations of the climb by cutting off or denying their feelings. This results in men treating people as objects. For some men, the struggle for power is so important that they use only the most basic of tools to accomplish their goals. They typically reward or punish others through the giving or withholding of material objects (pay-raises, fringe benefits, and special assignments). They seldom use the power of their expertise or their interpersonal relationship with their coworkers as a method of influence. Ironically, many men find that their influence on others is minimal.

Psychologists believe that people experiencing stress revert or regress to more simple, childlike, or even primitive behavior. When men get so wrapped up in the race for the top, stress causes them to rely on old behavior that is only minimally effective and effective with only a few people. Many men in the work-place, I believe, are in an almost constant state of stress. The result is that they threaten, bribe, or in some way treat people as objects.

To further complicate the situation, men are totally unaware of their machine-like manner toward others. Even when someone close to them tells them of their behavior, men deny the validity of the charge. One way that a man can gain awareness of his behavior is through a shock. One example of a shock is when a man receives a negative evaluation at work that threatens to slow or stop his progress in his career.

Stan received a startling evaluation at work in which his supervisor described his behavior as "insensitive, demanding, and unreasonable" with the people who worked under him. This behavior was not only unacceptable but also cast doubt about his future at the company. Stan had been able to ignore earlier and more subtle feedback. Now, he has begun to examine his behavior, but only because his career had been clearly and dramatically threatened.

Stan's wife confirmed that her husband often told her how frustrated he was at work. She believed that it was likely that he could be insensitive and intolerant at work because she had seen him behave that way at home. With two consistent sources of information about his behavior, Stan decided that he ought to examine his actions in light of this feedback. It's unfortunate that men need such a jolt to get their attention, but they seem to need a very hard bump to startle them into awareness.

In summary, the man in middle adulthood, especially in the beginning part of it, is strongly bent on achievement and advancement. He becomes enmeshed with his work; that is, his need for power becomes expressed through his role as worker, and this role takes precedence over roles such as spouse, father, sibling, son, or friend, which are roles that can bring about intimacy. This lack of balance leads inevitably to a decline in interpersonal relationships, an absence of emotional responsiveness, a growing sense of fatigue (often depression) and withdrawal or outbursts of energy in high-risk activities (hang-gliding, motorcycling), an increase in socially inappropriate behavior (excessive drinking, drug use, or gambling), and the appearance of physical symptoms (intestinal disorders or hypertension). Men can become machines no matter what their style of moving through middle adulthood and need help if they're going to avoid burnout.

The solution is easy to prescribe but difficult to implement. Men must first step back and get a fresh view of this life that's become unbalanced. There are numerous seminars that are offered to help them do this as part of the growing awareness in business and industry that men who are too involved with their work are not as productive as those who are more balanced in their lives. In this stepping-back process men come to grips with their basic error in thinking that more time and energy spent in work will gain more security and satisfaction for them.

Chapter Seven

When Climbing the Ladder Becomes Too Tiring

The Social Scene

Investment is the theme of the middle adulthood man at work and in social relationships. Most men attempt to establish, however ineffectively, a solid set of relationships that will enable them to feel connected to something other than their work. Relationships are the opposite of their career achievements. Relationships provide the touches and tender looks that say "I care about you" or "You're important to me." As most men begin middle adulthood, they have an intuition that they need some form of affiliation with others, such as a spouse or friends but aren't sure how to sustain these affiliations should they establish them. That is the challenge of the middle adulthood period.

It isn't easy

Most men say that they had more time for friends and their wives (if married) in early adulthood than in middle adulthood. Perhaps they got too wrapped up in the establishment of themselves as a success that they stopped trying to achieve intimacy. Here are three categories of social activities that men drop during middle adulthood.

1. Playing any group sport that takes more than two people per side. Men say that it is too difficult to find more than one other person.

2. Doing anything spontaneously. Men don't call up someone to do something that same day or evening because middle adulthood men are planful. They have a schedule of errands, meetings, work, night school, or a favorite television program. Others have a monthly card game, a weekly bowling league, or a Friday night dinner out. Men almost never drop over to a friend's house unannounced. As much as men would profit from socialization, planfulness drives out spontaneity.

I believe that spontaneity is important to men's mental health. Men become less and less impulsive as they grow older, it seems, and the lack of acting on their instincts destroys a creative and dynamic force that they can use in work and family situations. Men who become too planful lose the impulsive and childlike desire to have fun, make contact with others, and explore new relationships.

A confident man seeking intimacy with others said with much frustration, "I've got two small kids, but I'm still a little crazy and like to have a good time. I can't stand my uptight neighbors who are completely into money and style. Why can't they let go and have some fun? You know, just be real and emotional rather than stuffy. We're all just people!"

3. Doing anything alone or in a group that is not a group of couples. Middle adulthood men get married and then attend social events only with their spouse. One exception is when men go to a convention. I know of a group of men friends who meet each year at a conference. They eat meals together as well as attend concerts, plays, and athletic events. Strangers who see them say, "Are you in town for a convention?" Apparently that's the only reason middle adulthood men in this country are allowed to go out together other than to compete with each other in athletic contests.

Healthy social contact should provide communication with others, including the spontaneous expression of feelings and sharing new ideas and opinions. Unfortunately, a lot of barriers prevent this exchange from happening. One such barrier is geographical movement to new areas.

The movement from job to job within a field and the resulting move to a new home in a new neighborhood is a stressful event. Although men think little about a move, it uproots them from the familiar and comfortable and drops them into the unknown. Each time men move they face the awkward situation of meeting new neighbors and deciding if they can become friends. Even though a man may like the new residence, assimilation into a neighborhood is always difficult. Many men don't try to join their neighborhood and instead adopt a life of isolation.

A related issue is that many men do not wish to get close to people because they or their friends may move away. Never establishing closeness with someone avoids the pain of separating from that person. A graduate student and his wife knew that they would only be living in an area for three years and discussed this issue with me. They decided that they needed the friendship of those around them no matter what the pain would be later on. They made friends even though they knew that they would probably never again see these friends after graduation.

It isn't easy to meet intimacy needs in a society where power is so highly valued. It is easy to become overinvolved in work. I remember reading that career success leads to career satisfaction but not life satisfaction. In other words, a man who is successful at work reports that he's satisfied with his job, but he does not say that he's satisfied with his life.

I believe researchers who say that men who are the least successful and men who are the most successful at work are the least satisfied with their marriages. In order to give their marriages a chance to survive and to help them gain greater satisfaction with life, men must detach themselves from their work. No one can be satisfied with his job alone and expect to be satisfied with his entire life.

What's the cost of having a balance between power and intimacy? One cost is that a man wonders if he could have accomplished more at work if he'd have been more involved. This nagging thought precedes the regrets and second-guessing that often occur at the later part of middle adulthood, perhaps at forty, fifty, or sixty.

These men who balanced power and intimacy might have accomplished a lot more at work, but it would have been at a great cost to their families. In some cases men are already working at a point of diminishing returns, and so any additional involvement at work would make them less successful. One man who chose to ignore warnings from family and friends about over-involvement at work found that he had to take a lot of time off a few years later for his divorce, children's school failures, and psychological care. In most cases, such as this, relationships probably decline gradually and become little more than acquaintanceships.

The thrill is gone

Men lament, "I'm in a rut, and I don't know how to get out." On one hand, men want to have a secure niche and comfortable patterns that provide security as a result of their predictability. In other words, a man feels secure if he knows what to expect. Unfortunately, the patterns that bring about security can become ruts. The sameness of any pattern lulls people into emotional blandness. The feelings are there, but they're buried. One of two typical responses to this emotional boredom develops: continued decline or escape.

Escape from a rut in order to restore the thrill can take a number of forms, but for escape to be successful, a man must first be aware that he's in a rut, and then he must escape to something constructive. The key word here is awareness. The man who realizes that he's over-invested in a search for power and suffering from too little intimacy can make a planned escape. Too many unplanned escapes take the form of drugs or alcohol, a social frenzy, a sexual affair, or a sudden job shift. These types of escapes are doomed to failure because they don't address the problem. They cover it up. Only a man who carefully considers the demands on him and the toll these demands take can construct a workable escape plan. A number of healthy and workable plans exist, and they all involve an increase of emotional and intellectual stimulation.

Of course, some men have a higher need for stimulation than others, so their balance between security and stimulation will be different from other men. For example, one man reported to me that he enjoys going out to eat at a particular restaurant and having the same waitress, playing cards once a month with the same couples, and driving to and from work by the same route. Another man replied that he always wants to go to new restaurants, infrequently commits himself to a regular gathering of people, and often drives to and from work by different routes. Each of these men has a different balance between routine and stimulation. They each need a balance that works for them.

To gain more intellectual and emotional stimulation some men seek out new activities that may lead them into either relationships with new people or new relationships with current friends. Unfortunately, most men think that an activity by itself will pull them out of the rut. Hang-gliding, mountain climbing, and windsurfing are exciting, but the excitement wears off. Only the excitement that comes from people in intimate relationships is consistently refreshing. However, when men begin a new activity, they sometimes become more involved with new people by chance or in new ways with others who are already their friends, thus leading them into more satisfying relationships and out of their rut.

At a party with her husband, Randy, Sarah described her angry feelings toward her adolescent son to her married friends, Marge and Henry.

Sarah said, "I hollered at him (the son) for getting a tattoo, and then Randy told me to shut up, that I was making things worse."

Marge replied, "When my son wanted to get a tattoo, I stayed calm outwardly and said it was his decision, but he better be ready for some negative opinions from his teachers and maybe even from some of his friends."

Henry spoke up in contrast and said, "When I heard our son mention the tattoo and after hearing Marge talk to him, I was so upset I couldn't talk. I went upstairs and laid down in bed trying to read and listen to the radio. I wasn't mad, just so disappointed and confused and detached from him."

Sarah jumped back in laughing and said, "Henry, you're more like me emotionally, and Marge is more like Randy." A few minutes later, Henry was still thinking about Sarah's last observation. He said, "I never thought about it, but Marge and my family have always said that I get upset too easily, fly off the handle, worry too much. What Sarah said has me thinking that I may just be more emotionally sensitive and expressive than other men are and maybe like a lot of women. Maybe Marge is more like the typical "under-control" man."

Reflection can provide stimulation that leads men out of a social rut. It can end the boredom and malaise that often overtake them, but also can lead them to be fearful of change. Let's turn now to the marital relationship and how the middle adulthood man views it.

The price of responsibility

Part of the appeal of responsibility, in addition to meeting cultural expectations, is that taking responsibility meets needs for power. "I took on a challenge, and I'm happy that I've done it well", is often heard. But when men are able to let down their defenses, perhaps when they're in a psychologist's office, they begin to realize that the responsibility they'd accepted so casually on their natural progression into adulthood carries with it the fear that they might fail. I believe that any responsibility that a man takes on is accompanied by a fear of failure.

One man confided, "I never feel as if I can take a break or let down. It's a competitive world, and what I did yesterday doesn't mean anything today." Another man felt "scared" and that he "always had to plan for what might happen if he got sick or had an accident."

Not only do men fear failure but also they often resent that they're carrying the whole burden of responsibility of being the protector and provider. Resentment can be seen in statements such as, "Why am I working so hard? All my wife does is spend it" or "I'm tired of going out every day to earn a living and not having any help", or "My wife could help out more by working full-time, but she doesn't want to leave her part-time job." All of these statements were made by men who feel burdened and angry.

Many men respond to the fear of failure by using the emotional shutdown technique at the end of a tiring day. The man who says, "I've had a rough day, and all I want to do is relax," wants to turn off the feelings aroused during the day in the hope that a "shutdown" will make him feel better. A "shutdown" will help in the short run but will be destructive in the long run because "shutdowns" are based on the defense mechanisms of denial and avoidance. These two primitive coping behaviors don't work well on accumulated distress.

Furthermore, the "emotional shutdown" serves to shut out spouse and friends who are valuable resources for coping with emotions. The only release that these men will allow themselves is sex. Sex is a way for the middle adulthood man to release some of the day's tension and to feel better about himself.

Learning to be appropriately irresponsible

In order to handle the stress of responsibility in middle adulthood, to escape the ruts of work and social life, and to replenish their energy, men must learn to be "appropriately irresponsible." To be irresponsible means to act in child-like ways that are playful, frivolous, and what others would call "silly." "Silly" is the opposite of serious, and responsibility demands seriousness. However, acting child-like is not acting childish. Acting child-like means to behave with carefree exuberance and spontaneous emotion. To act childish means to act insensitively and in a self-centered way that ignores the wishes and feelings of others.

"Appropriately irresponsible" means that a man behaves irresponsibly without offending or embarrassing others. At a yearly conference I heard several men say that they had not laughed so hard or so often since the previous conference.

One man revealed "I like to go the park with my kids because I get to go down the slide and swing on the swings. I could never do that without my kids. I'd be too embarrassed. And I'd probably be arrested!" Another man said, "I would never go to the movies by myself, so I'm lucky that my brother visits me regularly. He and I enjoy doing things together like we did when we were kids."

It's tough for many men to be appropriately irresponsible because there's always something that they believe that they *should* be doing such as raking leaves, changing the furnace filters, or putting photographs into an album. The "shoulds" can kill men, because many men feel guilty if they do something they'd *like* to do instead of doing what they think they *should* be doing.

One difficulty in behaving appropriately irresponsible is the concern in the minds of many men that such behavior is selfish. If a man labels himself as selfish then guilt feelings emerge. This is a labeling problem. Men mislabel themselves as selfish. In my view, selfish is doing something that prevents someone else from doing something that he or she wants to do. For example, if a man goes to the gym on Monday evenings and it prevents his wife from going to dinner with an old friend who's passing through town, then he's probably being selfish. However, if going to the gym means that he's not helping his wife with the children for that evening when he helps every other night then he's not being selfish. Men must do more for themselves and risk mislabeling themselves as selfish. It's difficult for men to follow the advice of a man in a distant state who ended a recent telephone conversation with a man friend by saying, "Take care of your whole self."

Even if a man has gotten through the ruts and responsibility with a marriage that is somehow functional, he often faces role changes that are precipitated by his wife.

When a wife makes a change

Some men encounter the strain caused by a wife who wants to make changes in her life, unintentionally resulting in a threat to his sense of being powerful in their marriage. When a woman says that she is going to work outside the home, take a college class, or hire someone to do the housework, men feel threatened. They mistakenly believe that their wives no longer believes in their ability to carry out the role relationship that they have established. The desire of his wife for some self-satisfaction or personal development often feels like a criticism.

Other than the men who attack their wives and try to restore the status quo, many men blame themselves. Other men hold out false hope that in time "she'll change back." Men must accept that these changes are likely to be a permanent pattern of growth for their wives and to begin to accept it.

As one man said, "I had to start making the bed, which I hadn't done for eleven years, and without asking for a medal for it." A similar man recalled, "The biggest thing for me to accept was that the household chores and the shopping for the kids' clothes and all the other stuff was for both of us to do and not divided into "hers" and "mine" the way it was with my parents." Another man remarked, "I found it difficult to support her in her activities where I thought she would fail and be disappointed." Although I work with couples to help men support and accept the changes that their wives make, some men become completely passive and dependent wimps who often are resented by the women they want to please.

Don't be a wimp

In some cases a man who has been the typical strong silent type fears that his wife's new roles (and the loss of his roles) means that she no longer needs him and that she'll eventually leave him. A panic sets in, and the man tries either to convince her to return to the "way we used to be" in a show of force or throws himself on her mercy in a show of dependence. He loses either way because his tough guy role was what she rejected in the first place and his completely acquiescent side disgusts her. Just because she doesn't want him to be a protector doesn't mean that she wants him to be a baby.

The answer is for men to be patient. It's like a pendulum. At one end of the swing a man is an independent person who wants his wife to be completely dependent on him so he'll feel powerful. On the opposite arc as the pendulum swings, a man is a dependent little boy who's frightened that he'll be abandoned and powerless.

The pendulum can settle somewhere in the middle. It just takes time to get there. It helps if both husband and wife realize what's happening.

The answer for men is to admit when they feel scared and lonely, frustrated and angry, as well as tired and weak, and hope to find someone to make them feel better. When a man starts to expect a woman to put a band-aid on him, he's in danger of being a wimp. He's got to coach his wife to support him without patronizing him or ignoring him completely. Hopefully, he'll convince her that he can be vulnerable without falling apart, sensitive without being immobilized, and affective without being irrational.

Chapter Eight

Changing Partners

Sometimes men decide to divorce and to "start over." This painful process will alter the course of a man's life in significant and long-lasting ways. The end results of the divorce vary, but the divorce itself is always painful. If a man felt powerless in his marriage then the divorce will make him feel even worse.

Marriage Burnout

The typical man in this group has been married for seven to ten years, has established himself in his career, has several children, considerable financial debt, and is tired. Tired is the word that is often used to describe many men in middle adulthood, especially those who divorce at this time.

In early adulthood a man may have married a woman before he was emotionally prepared, thus leading to a rude awakening and a divorce. One man in middle adulthood told me that he made the right decision to marry, but now thinks that he's used up his emotional resources and has little left to give to his wife and children. He's the opposite of the man who blames his wife for not having enough energy, or the motivation to use the energy she has, to restore him. He believes in the "battery" theory of interpersonal relationships. Just as a battery runs out of energy, many men feel that they have run out of emotional energy. Some batteries can be recharged in a fairly easy and efficient manner, but most men are unlikely to know how to recharge themselves and are often unaware that they are becoming drained. The task becomes one of helping men to recognize the signs of emotional fatigue and then to help them to recharge themselves.

The signs of emotional drain are 1) decreased interest in socialization, 2) excessive fatigue where additional sleep does not seem to have an impact, 3) lack of concentration at home as indicated by forgetfulness, and 4) quite often, but not always, an increased interest in some new challenge such as weight loss or smoking cessation, or even a hobby such as jogging, home improvement, a musical instrument, or a computer. These signs of emotional burnout are self-evident as being indicators of some distress, except for an increased interest in a new challenge. Most wives look upon an increase in interests as a positive sign, but it may be a case of too little too late.

New leisure activities are a good sign for the man who has recognized that he is too involved in seeking power, and needs some leisure activities that make him feel challenged and competent. However, many men begin these activities far after they have burned out and are preparing to leave their family. It's as if once they have made their decision to end the relationship, they discover a burst of energy and use this energy to take on a new activity in preparation for their exit. Other men need an activity to lean on once they have left their secure environment. A man in this position described to me, "Once I made the decision in my own mind to leave, I felt relieved. I was scared and embarrassed, but definitely relieved." Men who recognize these signs may be able to make some corrections in their lives and avoid the necessity of leaving a relationship in order to regain their energy supply. It is not necessary to divorce in order to become recharged. There's a lot more energy available if only men knew how to access it.

But what about the man who is aware of his distress and wants to do something but doesn't know what it is that he should do? He could receive professional help, particularly in the form of group counseling with other men who are in a similar life struggle. In addition, this man needs a new marital contract in which more of his needs are met. This contract can be negotiated with the help of a counselor who specializes in counseling couples. However, the first step is to reduce the number of "shoulds" that he faces.

This man needs to stop pushing himself to attain power, because it's this quest that drains him of so much emotional energy and returns so little to him. For many men a first step means that they reduce their workload. For others it means limiting their outside activities and hobbies.

The best way to get a busy man away from his scramble for the top is to build in some time away from his work with the entire family and some time just with his wife. This relaxation period should be scheduled on a regular and frequent basis. Weekends will have events planned beginning with Friday night dinner at a restaurant without the kids. One couple made this Friday night dinner a ritual, which probably helped their marriage survive, as the man was struggling to establish himself in a law practice. Another man went away with his wife one weekend each month even if it was only Saturday night, at a nearby motel. A third man spent every Friday night eating pizza and watching rented movies with his wife while his answering machine took any telephone calls. All of these men have been able to have a successful career and a satisfying marriage.

Many men have made dramatic changes in their lives during middle adulthood. Not all men do, but enough make changes proving that men at this life stage have the ability to make an abrupt and long-lasting shift in the balance between power and intimacy.

Joint Custody

Divorced fathers often become involved in a power struggle over custody with their ex-spouse. It doesn't matter who starts the power struggle; however, withdrawing from the conflict often means that men must withdraw from their children. There are several ways for both parents to remain actively involved in the lives of their children; however, the potential for conflict is high in almost all situations.

The method of child custody that has the least long-term conflict is sole custody by one of the parents, usually the mother. When one parent is in charge, she (or sometimes he) doesn't have to consult with the other parent at all. The non-custodial parent has little to say about any aspect of the raising of the children.

Joint custody means that both parents share in all aspects of raising their children, although the children usually have a primary home (often with the mother) and a secondary home (often with the father). This method is fraught with conflict because the father may give opinions about the child's life, but his ex-wife doesn't necessarily accept these opinions. The frustration leads to arguments, legal actions, and very often the father gives up and drops out of the children's lives. I believe that about fifty percent of the divorced fathers without full custody of their young children stop seeing them completely within three years after the divorce. It's too difficult to keep up a long distance relationship with a child, especially when it's one in which a man must continually fight with his ex-wife.

It's also difficult for fathers when their children withdraw from them. Children of divorced parents, especially younger children, feel abandoned by the parent who moves out of the home. Children have trouble understanding that the parent who moved away from them still loves them. The child's confusion and possible wariness can cause the absent parent to become discouraged at trying to convince the child of his love. If the father stops seeing the children then the children are left to believe that their fears were true.

Dr. Janice Roberts-Wilbur, a psychologist who works with families, has allowed me to present her ten double binds (no-win situations) common to what she calls the "throw-away" parent. The throw-away parent is the one who is not given custody of the children and in most cases is the father. Here are Dr. Wilbur's dilemmas that are typical of these men:

> 1. They are considered to be irresponsible if they don't pay child support but are criticized for trying to buy the children.
>
> 2. If they don't see the children they are labeled a bad parent, but if they do see the children they are criticized for being a bad influence.

3. If the children are doing well the parent feels unimportant, but if they are not doing well the parent feels guilty.
4. They are told they are not important as parents but are blamed for any problems that the children have.
5. They are criticized for not caring or being more informed about the children but are not informed by their ex-wife of anything that is going on in the children's lives.
6. If they try to plan ahead then they are refused permission to see the children, but if they don't plan ahead they can't see the children because they didn't let the custodial parent know far enough ahead of time.
7. If they work then they are criticized for caring more about their career than their children, but if they don't work then they are criticized for not providing financially for the children.
8. They are criticized for being a weekend "Disneyland" parent but are excluded from any day-to-day contact with the children.
9. They are told to wait until the children get older but are criticized for not doing anything about the present situation.
10. They are told that child support and visitation are separate but are not permitted to see the children if they don't pay the support.

I believe that the best approach for a man and his ex-wife who have resolved their anger toward each other is co-parenting. Co-parenting means that fathers are actively involved in the regular weekly activities of their children, including housing them. In one variation of this model the children live for part of the week at one parent's home and part of the week at the other parent's home. In this way there is a regular and agreed-upon pattern of living arrangements, which reduces the power struggle between parents and the ambiguity among the children. One child said, "It's nice at my Dad's house, and it's nice at my Mom's house. It's sort of like having two houses. I go to the same school so my friends are the same no matter which house I'm in."

Some people contend that a shift between two residences is confusing and somehow detrimental to the children, but I've heard a number of anecdotes that report that children thrive in this arrangement. Children do best, I believe, if they have a stable and loving relationship with both parents, even parents who don't care much for each other and are divorced. Living in two different households is irrelevant when children are with caring parents.

Miriam Galper has nicely described the specifics of co-parenting in *Joint Custody and Co-Parenting*. The details of establishing a co-parenting arrangement are thoroughly covered.

Separation

When couples stop trying to meet their needs with each other, they separate. Some separations result in divorce, but I've read that most separations result in reconciliation. Therefore, separation should be viewed in terms of what it can do for a relationship instead of seeing it as an inevitable step toward divorce. If anger can be reduced then there's a chance for intimacy to be established.

Usually the middle adulthood man has not met his needs for power at work and intimacy needs with his wife and takes out his frustration and disappointment on his wife in the form of anger. A man who is relatively oblivious to the cause of his distress usually turns to the person closest to him and vents his frustration on her. The paradox is that the man pushes away his closest ally and so removes the only consistent resource on whom he can rely.

However, many men do not show their distress by outward displays of anger such as fighting, staying away from home, or decreased interest in sex. Some men may do the opposite. These men want to get out of the relationship but believe that they are at fault and feel guilty about it. They feel guilty but somehow powerless to correct themselves. Therefore, they act very kind, generous, and interested. Inside they are preparing to leave physically and have already left psychologically.

Unfortunately, most separations take place with little or no planning and when both partners are very upset with each other. This situation leads to husband and wife having few expectations of getting together again; therefore, they don't use the separation in any way that could help their marriage. During most separations, couples typically spend money foolishly and incur unnecessary debts, begin to date and have sex with a variety of other people, and fail to raise their kids adequately. Separated couples often find an attorney to file for a divorce and take other steps that make their spouse even more hurt and angry. I recommend that separated couples consult an attorney, but only to gain information about the law and not to begin divorce proceedings.

Furthermore, separated couples often tell their friends that their spouse is the "bad guy" and tell the kids the same thing. All of these actions move the man and woman into an adversarial position. It's difficult to get back together once husband and wife become opponents.

In order to arrange a separation that might bring about a reconciliation, couples should determine how long the separation should last, who will tell their kids, family, and friends, who will pay the bills and other financial matters, and if they will date others and have sex with these other people. Even if the separated couple decides to divorce, a negotiated separation will make the divorce and subsequent interactions over the children more amicable.

How long?

Overall, a qualified and experienced counselor can be of great help in assisting a couple with these negotiations. Separating couples must think of the separation as time-limited; that is, the separation will go on as long as it's effective. Most effective separations are more than a week but less than six months, in my experience. Returning too soon will guarantee that the couple will return to their old destructive pattern and probably split permanently at a later time.

A separation must last long enough to disrupt the old and unproductive habits into which the couple has fallen and allow the man's need for intimacy to surface. Each person must become aware of how they feel now that his or her partner has gone. Men must think about what these feelings mean. Some men feel lonely and distressed while others feel relieved and energized. Men need time to think about their partner and themselves in an un-pressured way that just isn't possible while living together in daily conflict.

I suggest that the first two weeks should be a cooling-off period. During this time, the couple should have as little contact with each other as possible. This will allow each person to calm down from the distress that preceded the separation. In some cases the burnout is so extensive that little distress was experienced before the split, and this cooling-off period may be shortened. In most cases the man and woman need some time to let their distress subside and begin to think about the marriage.

During the separation, the goal is to make the relationship more businesslike or formal. For example, from the time that the husband leaves, he must consider his wife to be the sole resident in their home. He must call before he comes over rather than stop by unannounced and knock when he wishes to enter the house. Men have a big problem with this guideline, but the formality creates a barrier that can keep the anger from being expressed. In addition, it might establish a new feeling of respect for their wives.

At the end of this period, if the couple is sufficiently calmed down, they should start to date each other. They should do things together that will be fun and relaxing for both of them. In this way they may begin to enjoy each other's company enough to rebuild their relationship and regain the intimacy that was lost or never experienced. Specifically, they should go out together rather than stay at home and watch television. Initially, I recommend that couples go out no more than once a week. This can be increased as their comfort with each other progresses. They should not talk about their problems no matter what their partner does to initiate such a conversation. In this way they will have a chance to re-establish enough rapport to begin the task of reopening the intimate side of their relationship.

A separated man reported, "It was tough going on a date with Lorraine after being married. At first we talked only about the kids and gossip about our friends and neighbors. It was like we had just met and were trying to please each other. I guess we hadn't been on good behavior with each other for a long time. I know I bit my tongue several times, and I'm sure she did too. I wanted the separation, and I felt distant from her for years. Now I felt as though I really looked forward to seeing her and she seemed pleased to spend time with me too."

The dating phase may not go smoothly, and each person should meet with his or her marriage counselor or psychologist on an individual basis every week. This helps each person to adjust to his or her new life situation and to identify the problems that led to the separation.

After the dating phase, which may take weeks or months, the couple may begin to discuss their problems together with their counselor once or twice a week. They should continue dating and maybe increase the frequency of the dates. However, they should keep the dates separate from the discussion time. Basically, the strategy is to have them resolve old issues and find solutions in the counseling office while having some time to enjoy each other outside of counseling.

The separated man who spoke about dating went on to say, "The stuff we discussed was really painful, and I could barely keep my mouth shut when we went out together, but I did. Gradually, I began to feel less ignored or else less justified in feeling ignored. I also felt less defensive."

The next phase is the preparation for re-entry phase. In this phase the couple discuss how life will be different when they reconcile. A helpful technique is to write down the new arrangement that they wish to implement. It's impossible to be too concrete at this stage. Examples of new behavior are: to go out to dinner together each Friday night for the next three months, to spend less money on home decorating, (or to spend more money on home decorating), to take more time/less time with relatives, to share household chores, to name a few, that represent the ways that problems have emerged into their day-to-day activities. I believe that these activities only address the symptom of the problems and not the problems themselves. The problems such as feelings of a lack of power and/or intimacy and other problems must be resolved in joint meetings between the couple and their counselor. Once again the separated man says, "This part was easy to do, because I'm very specific and detailed. I like having everything spelled out. The really hard part was to realize how we had patterns that we'd learned as kids to protect ourselves emotionally from the frustration and disappointment of our lives as workers and parents. We really expected too much from our relationship."

Next is the reconciliation phase. Here the man moves back in, the couple begins to recover from the separation, and they attempt to implement the knowledge and strategies that they have learned. They should continue to work with their counselor on a regular basis even though many want to stop at this point. A vacation from therapy is in order only if it can be combined with a traditional vacation. This is the time when many couples should go on a vacation together. The worst time to take a vacation together, in my opinion, is when the couple is close to separation or divorce and thinks that spending time together will somehow make their relationship improve. Although taking a vacation to circumvent divorce apparently is conventional wisdom among many couples, I think that they usually have an unpleasant time and will want to separate even more intensely than before.

Who tells whom?

A big question that arises after a couple decides to separate is who will tell children, parents and friends. I urge couples with children to tell the children together. Usually each person is hesitant to tell other people because of embarrassment in the case of friends and fear of criticism in the case of parents. Nevertheless, the couple also is likely to fear that their partner will not be fair or accurate in his/her presentation of the reasons for the separation. Therefore, the couple should divide the list of friends and agree about what will be said to them. The safest strategy is to tell no more than that there's been a mutual agreement about a separation due to mutual dissatisfaction. It may last for a few months and hopefully will result in reconciliation. Each person can tell his/her own parents the same story.

Friends won't press for more information and those who do are not real friends and should be ignored. Family may press for more details, but they can be avoided until after the cooling-off period when the issues can be discussed more calmly. Every couple about to separate is worried over what his or her partner will say to their friends and family. Agreeing on what will be said eliminates a lot of bad feelings that would otherwise occur.

Unfortunately, men seem to like to have their wives tell everyone and so are slow in telling the friends and relatives on their list. This forces their wives to answer questions and handle phone calls from the people whom her husband was supposed to notify. This behavior of the husband creates additional resentment among wives. One honest man admitted, "I just didn't want to admit to my friends that I was another divorce statistic. It was easier for them to find out from other people, and some of them avoided mentioning it to me even though I know that they knew."

Money?

The first question is where can a man afford to move? If money is an issue, he can move in with a friend or relative who will let him stay free or at a low cost. Too many men refuse to move out because of embarrassment and use money as the excuse. This refusal hardens the wife's resistance and increases the likelihood of a divorce.

The next issue is how the couple will divide their income in order to meet each of their expenses. They should postpone all but the most necessary expenditures and make a budget to which each will agree to live by during the separation. This means canceling home improvements, clothing purchases, cars, and anything that would strain the family budget. The person who did the banking, bill-paying, and other money matters can continue to do this job but must keep the other person informed.

Dating and sex?

A big concern of both men and women is whether their spouse will date and have sex with other people. Dating other people and having sex with them is a bad idea. Separated people who are serious about their relationship (either in restoring it or in ending it) must have a clear head during this time. No one can handle two relationships effectively at one time.

It's a great boost to the ego to be asked out or to have someone accept an invitation to go out, but dating without feelings is impossible, and feelings need to be straightened out during a separation. Feelings that get stirred up during dating confuse people far more than the ego boost is worth. Usually people say that they are just interested in having someone to talk to, but it never ends there.

Remarriage

The divorced mid-life man is likely to remarry sometime during this period. The single-life loneliness, the right woman, and the children (his and his prospective partner's) will all help to determine if he will remarry.

Single-life loneliness

This is the biggest determinant of whether a man will remarry or not, I believe. The relief of being out of an unhappy marriage will soon wear off, and he may soon tire of the excitement of dating. Once the divorced man in middle adulthood feels lonely, he will begin the search for another wife. Unfortunately, he's not in the best emotional state to make a wise choice. Remarrying to feel less lonely is not a very good reason. It's a factor in every marriage, but if it's the primary reason then the risk of a bad choice looms large.

As one man painfully revealed, "I know now that I remarried too soon. Sue's a nice person, but she wanted someone to support her kids and herself financially. I guess I was just too lonely and didn't realize how my feelings could affect my judgment so much. I'm usually an excellent judge of people. Now I'm in a marriage that I want to get out of."

How does a man tell if loneliness is too much of a factor in remarriage? Talk to friends and see what they think. Talk to a counselor too. If a man doesn't have many friends and has trouble being by himself then he should learn to live by himself before he reenters a marital relationship.

I recommend that every divorced man wait at least a year before entering a serious relationship with a potential partner. Don't just wait a year to remarry. Wait a year to get serious with anyone. Waiting less than a year increases the risk of making a poor decision. After a divorce, a lot of healing and growing needs to be accomplished, and it takes time.

Once men are divorced, they're in a new world. They'll change in ways that they could not have predicted. Some men will have had their defenses stripped away, and they'll be emotionally reactive to everything. They may withdraw and hide until their defenses get stronger, or they may use their emotions to build new ways of relating to people. Other men will have increased the size of their defensive shield in order to avoid being hurt again. They'll invest in work or other activities so as not to get involved with women again.

The man who's had his defenses blown off and keeps them from re-forming to their prior level will have a better marriage the second time around. The man who rebuilds his defenses quickly is likely to remarry quickly and often to the same type of woman he first married, in my observation. The highly-defended man will be unlikely to remarry. It's too big of a risk for him.

What will men face as they re-enter the potential marriage market? Some feel that it's just exactly that, a market. They find that there are a lot of women looking for a husband. Some men like the attention and others get scared by it. Some men try to find the right woman, while other men just try to find someone with whom to spend the night.

The right woman

Finding the right woman could mean finding the opposite of the woman he just divorced or it could mean finding the woman his ex-wife was when he first married her. In the first case a man believes that he married someone who really wasn't what he wanted. Either he made an error in judging his ex-wife due to passion or immaturity, or else he married someone who changed in ways that he couldn't stand. In either case a man wanting to remarry looks for someone who meets his needs as he currently sees them. But what a man wants may not be what he needs.

What some men need is a woman who will be relatively submissive to their level of dominance (as motivated by insecurity and a need for power) and will be dependent upon them. But many of these men may believe that they want a strong, independent woman. Why does a man look for someone who isn't good for him? I think that the answer is ego. He asks for what he'd *like* to need. He'd like to be a man who can and would enjoy an independent woman. Unfortunately, when a man pretends to be someone he's not, he only fools himself.

The other characteristic (in addition to level of dominance) that men should look for in a woman to remarry is her level of emotional giving and receiving. Many men seem to need to have a wife who gives a lot and asks for very little. Men who are busy in their career and who are not going to make home a major theme of their lives need a woman who is content with minimal intimacy from her husband.

One particularly enlightened man stated, "I know now that I need a wife who feels and acts as if I'm important to her. Someone who thinks about what I want to do, where to go, and what matters to me. I don't care if she works, has friends, goes out to activities without me, but I want her to think about me, and I want her to show it."

The right woman for the mid-life man to remarry can be older, younger, of a different religion, race, or ethnic heritage, tall or short. These factors may have had a significant influence on the courtship and marriage that took place while the man was in early adulthood, but they make little difference now. Men have the potential to be less vulnerable to societal influence surrounding these factors. Middle adulthood men have the ability to focus on psychological characteristics rather than superficial physical features. Hopefully, these men will use their abilities to make a proper choice.

The only other important factor that some men think about when considering a second marriage is money. Does this woman have an income or an inheritance that will allow him to have the same lifestyle that he did when he was living on his own? Is she willing to work if they need the income to let them live the way they want to live? All of this is a way for a man to determine how much of a protector and provider role he must play.

Her children and his children

Many divorced men in middle adulthood who begin to date encounter women who are divorced and have children. Dating divorced women used to be a big issue and may still be one for some men. In the past, men who met divorced women wondered who was at fault in the break-up of the marriage of this seemingly normal woman. They worried that this divorced woman might change after the remarriage. It's an irrational fear, and one that seems to have diminished among many men. There are so many divorced women now that divorced men need to get used to the idea of children being in the picture. Kids are quite another story.

One scenario shows the divorced man who has no children or has children living with his ex-wife. He meets a woman who has one or more small children from her previous marriage. Some men are not looking for a family, just a wife. Consequently, these men drop a woman with children as soon as they hear the phrase, "my kids." They're afraid to take on the responsibility of raising and relating to children who are unknown to them. It's difficult enough to get to know the woman let alone her kids. They also fear that they won't have a significant role or power with this woman's children after marriage because they are *her* children, not his.

The man who is put off by a woman who has children may underestimate how well he will be able to establish a family that will be satisfying to him. He won't ever be the biological father to the children, but he could be an excellent father on a day-to-day basis. Day-to-day fatherhood is better than biological fatherhood every time. He won't have had the chance to influence the child's early years, but there's plenty of time left. Men need to overcome these fears if they are to be successful at this second marriage.

Another scenario shows a divorced man who has custody of his children and meets a woman who has custody of her children. One might think that these people would be wary, but it doesn't seem to happen that way in my experience. On the contrary, men with children seem to find women with children more acceptable than do men without children. Are men with children more accepting? Are they just desperate to find a mother for their children? It's difficult to say what motivates them. Men with children seem motivated to blend families with little hesitation.

Another part of blending families is the man who remarries a woman who has children from her previous marriage, and he wants to have a child with her. This is more prevalent with men who have no children by their first wife. For some reason men without biological children who remarry want to have children "of their own." I believe this shows men to be more concerned with passing on their genes than caring for and nurturing children. I recommend that this issue be settled in counseling before marriage takes place.

All in all, there will be more marriages of mid-life men to women with children and more families with his children, her children, and their children than ever before in this country. It's confusing at first, but it all works out, probably because the children are so flexible and resilient.

The first part of middle adulthood is often a time for establishment, but for some men it's a time for ending a marriage and starting over. The paradox and the tragedy is that men who try hardest to establish themselves at work seem most likely to become the victims of divorce. The most responsible of men are often the most emotionally controlled, which may lead to success at work but disaster in social relations. It's difficult to step back and see yourself as being off-balance, but many men do it. Balance between the needs for power and intimacy will bring about peace of mind that can help the middle adulthood man weather any storm and even grow from it.

Chapter Nine

Later Mid-life: Consolidation or Change?

Introduction

In contrast to the confidence that marked the start of early adulthood when a man believed that his hard work and skill would bring him everything wanted, the later part of middle adulthood is characterized by cautious anticipation of the demands of the future. The power he has attained can no longer block out the fears of what might be ahead.

I use the following guideline to chart the development of men according to age.
- Adolescence: teens to early 20's
- Early Adulthood: 20's to 30's (Transition to 30: late 20's)
- Middle Adulthood: 30's to 50's (Transition to 40: late 30's)

Age Progression

Men who consolidate their gains and move slowly from satisfying power needs to satisfying intimacy needs display one type of pattern of behavior during this period. A second pattern is found among men who make drastic changes in their lives resulting in a sharp decrease in interest in power and a dramatic increase in a search for intimacy.

The consolidation pattern is highlighted by long-term planning. These plans could include college for the children, job security that extends to retirement, a home that will be suitable for the next three decades, and satisfying relationships with spouse and friends. Men adopting this strategy feel confident but concerned, energetic but cautious, involved with others yet unconnected.

One man who consolidated reported, "For the first time in my life, I'm concerned about the future. I always thought that the future would take care of itself. What I mean is that I trusted my instinct to be able to handle whatever presented itself, good or bad. Now I think about putting money away to educate my kids, if they want to get more schooling after high school. I also want to have enough money put away to take care of my wife and me if we should have bad health problems or an accident, God forbid. I also want to take more time off and do things, travel, take a vacation to somewhere different, maybe Hawaii. I guess that I'm worried about the realistic parts of the future, and I'm going to do whatever it takes to make sure that I'm ready for them."

The drastic change pattern is noted by a sudden break with the past and creation of a new order of priorities of work and social life. Men who change make this point in time a turning point. They marry, or divorce and remarry, change jobs or retire early and start a new job, or make new friends. Men who change feel disappointed but hopeful, lonely but worthy of relationships, pressed by their stage in life but not panicked.

A man who changed instead of consolidating stated, "I guess that I finally realized that I felt unhappy no matter what I tried to do. I have no real friends, and now I want some. It's not that I want to be twenty-one again. I don't. I just want to get off the treadmill and really live. I know that I'm taking some big risks by moving to California, but I've got to try it."

Whether a man changes or consolidates depends on how powerful and how intimate with others he feels. Of course, men must first become aware of their level of satisfaction of power and intimacy needs. Most men sense a vague degree of satisfaction or dissatisfaction and then judge how powerful and how intimate they feel. Usually men in early adulthood or the early part of middle adulthood who feel dissatisfied decide that they don't have enough power. Men in the latter part of middle adulthood often decide that more power won't help and that their problem is lack of intimacy.

Along with a consolidation or a change in the latter part of middle adulthood is a shift from using thoughts exclusively as a way to evaluate one's reactions to life events to using feelings. Instead of reacting to an incident by thinking, "What do I *think* about that?" men are now more likely to ponder, "How do I *feel* about that?"

Men who move from thoughts toward feelings have probably been fatigued and frustrated in their search for power and now want to do something differently. Other men have felt power and the emptiness that accompanies it, so they now want something more fulfilling. All men will find that becoming aware of their feelings will make this part of middle adulthood a very new world.

A confident man said, "Being in my forties isn't bad at all, and I don't think I'll mind being in my fifties. But I think that I'll mind turning sixty because it will mean that I'm close to retirement. Right now, I feel in control and capable of handling what I see to be the things that will be required of me in the future." In response to a question about financial responsibility he said, "Financial demands are important, but I don't really feel that money is my big concern. I actually worry less about money than I did ten years or so ago. I may *think* about it as much, but I don't *worry* about it as much, if that makes sense."

Some psychologists say that when men admit that they stand approximately at the chronological midpoint of their lives, they begin to enter the latter part of mid-life. This awareness motivates them either to consolidate or to make changes. But they won't do much of anything if they deny that they are, indeed, near the midpoint. The following statements are typical of those made by men who refuse to recognize where they are in life.

"I'm too young to be that old."

The man who makes this statement means that he "feels" too young to be as old as he perceives other men at this age to be. If he doesn't accept his life stage as somewhere in middle adulthood, then he'll delay making either a consolidation or a change.

One man said that he felt fine being forty because he didn't intend to do anything any differently than he had done before. "After all," he said, "I'm in good physical shape, and I'm successful at what I do. I haven't changed much in the last ten years, and I don't intend to change very much in the next ten years." I believe that everyone changes, whether they want to or not, and this man is setting himself up for a shock that he will not be prepared to handle. He assumes that his world remains constant, which I believe is big mistake.

In my view, friends, family, and jobs always change, and these changes influence men in subtle but powerful ways. The man who resists change is living in an illusion that change is not affecting him. He may realize the changes when it's too late to do much about them. If he could admit his vulnerability to change all around him then he could begin to prepare himself for the future.

"I'm not ready to be 40."

Men who make this statement have not achieved the fantasy or plan that they devised in early adulthood. Unfortunately, they are not able to admit that they may never accomplish it, and that maybe the plan was an unreasonable one. It may have been based on an unrealistic assessment of their talents or on outside factors beyond their control. Right now, they feel disappointed that they weren't powerful enough to attain that dream.

One remedy for these feelings is to switch to another plan. The problem is that a man must become less ego-involved with the original one in order to accept a second one. Many men are invested in a particular plan (usually work) to the exclusion of other activities (family or friends). They place themselves in an all-or-nothing situation. If they carry out the plan then they win at life. If they don't accomplish it then they're a total failure. It's a high-risk situation. Like stockbrokers who say to diversify, men should have the same philosophy about their lives.

A man, who failed to be promoted to the position he had anticipated reflected a few years later, "I have to admit that I began to spend more time with my family and friends because I didn't get promoted. I was disappointed and depressed about the promotion at first. I knew that I would be in that same spot for the rest of my career. Actually, I'm glad in a way now that I didn't get the promotion because I've had a good time at home."

Paradoxically, many men who have completed their plan of wealth, power, or prestige are often very unhappy and dissatisfied. It seems that the dream of accumulating possessions and status brings happiness perhaps only rarely. It's a real blow when a man achieves his dream and then finds that it isn't worth very much.

"I'm too old to change."

When a man says that he's too old to change, he's scared to attempt a change. He fears that he will face stresses that will be difficult to handle, and he's probably right. One of the typical fears that a man in the later part of mid-life admits is not advancing any further in his career and the ongoing financial pressure to pay for increasing expenses of a family. Although this is an issue that men frequently identify, they will face many others that they are not aware of at this time. Such issues include the loss of children as they gain independence, decline of physical ability and especially sexual performance, the lack of a satisfying emotional relationship with a spouse, and the lack of anyone with whom they can really talk. An examination of these issues may prepare men to cope with them without a "mid-life crisis."

One man revealed blandly, "I don't think that I can or would do anything radically different in my career now. I can't afford to. Plus I'm not qualified to do anything else. I could go back to school I suppose, but who would hire me at my age when they could get a guy twenty years younger who they could pay a lot less than I would accept. No, I'm stuck here whether I like it or not."

In response to a question about his feelings toward his family and friends, he replied with some emotion, "I like my friends, and I wouldn't want to make new ones, say if we had to move or something. I like my family, but I know the kids are growing up quickly and won't be here too much longer. I wish that the kids would stay near us after they leave home. I wonder what it will be like for Kate and me then. We just sort of exist right now. We don't really talk or do much together except with the kids. I know she'd like me to talk more, but it's hard for me."

Let's examine the concerns men admit as well as those men don't.

Mid-life Problems

Career concerns

Earlier in life, men wondered whether or not they were in the career that would lead to success. They also feared that even if they were on the right track they might not have what it takes to compete with the others in the race. Men in the later part of middle adulthood look at their track record and wonder if they can or even want to continue on that same track "for the next thirty years", as one man remarked with concern in his voice.

It's not that they have been unsuccessful, but that they have lost a lot of their humanity and sensitivity in the way they have run the race and haven't gained the sense of satisfaction that they thought would come with power. The most financially successful man may be unhappy at his present state of who he is emotionally and interpersonally, and so he may change careers to feel better about himself. The financially unsuccessful man may be unhappy so then he changes careers for a last chance effort to achieve the power that he has not as yet attained. Of course, career problems have an impact on social relationships.

One man told of how he had to be deceptive and manipulative with the lawyers he opposed in court. He also had a tough time being honest at home. He didn't see the connection between the two. With effort in counseling he began to be more honest with his family and friends, and he began to be more straightforward at work. He may or may not become more effective at work, and actually he may be less successful with certain people, but now he feels better about himself. He's happier about his home life, and his wife and kids are happier with him.

Unfortunately, for every man who feels frustrated or disappointed and wants to cope with these feelings, there is another man who feels the same feelings and wants to avoid or deny them. However, many men don't believe that they will succeed unless they feel the pressure of the marketplace. Their motto is "No matter how well we did last month, we can always do better; so keep the pressure on." It's probably not until a man is told by his boss that he's been passed over for promotion or when he starts having physical symptoms that affect his job performance that the message sinks in.

Physical signs

Most men don't worry about their health until a problem prevents them from working or when someone challenges their image of themselves. Lower back pain after sitting, shortness of breath after climbing a flight of stairs or indigestion are signs to men that their bodies are less healthy than they used to be. Many men suffer through these times without doing much to help themselves. It may take a more severe incident such as a gall bladder attack, a week or two of bed rest for back spasms, or a hyperventilation scene before they do anything about their body. Sometimes it takes a heart attack.

Many men refuse to notice these warning signs until their performance at work is affected. When work is affected, men get scared. Fear is a powerful motivator. Men, who fear that they will not be able to work as much or as effectively as they had been doing, may start to take better care of themselves.

One man played softball for the first time in a decade. Although he is a regular jogger and a frequent visitor to a gym's weight room, he was sore for three days after the game to the point of missing a day of work. His response was to exercise in moderation when faced with an activity in which he rarely participated. He learned that his body couldn't do the things that it used to do without a very painful consequence.

But what about men's sensitivity to the natural and inevitable aging process? Do they fear that they'll be surpassed at work?

That's part of it, I believe. Many men fear that they will either lose their job or that someone younger will surpass them.

There are several other insights that physical changes bring about. One insight is that a man is closer to death than ever before, and the other is that he is not as sexually appealing as he used to be. Both of these insights diminish a man's feeling of power. He begins to question how powerful he really is in the case of approaching death. He begins to question the worth of his attractiveness to others in the case of loss of physical attributes.

Both awareness of death and diminishing sexual desirability show men how vulnerable they are. In adolescence men believe that they are invincible, and that death is a long way off. Slowly, they see that friends, family, and others die and that they are the next in an inescapable line. For many, it's not until they see in the mirror that they are closer in appearance to that of their father than that of their son that they realize their proximity to the end of life. Of course, how men choose to live with this knowledge is important. Some retrain and refit themselves while others plunge ahead without heeding the visible signs.

Attractiveness

Early in life men acquire the belief that being sexually attractive is synonymous with power and this guarantees a mate and will insure an effective role of protector and provider. Therefore, the loss of sexually attractive characteristics means the loss (in the minds of many men) of power, intimacy, and being a good protector and provider. I believe that men can be powerful, achieve intimacy and be an effective protector and provider without superficial physical characteristics. To do so, men must develop the interpersonal skills that help them be involved without being controlling, caring without being possessive, supportive without being smothering, and committed without being resentful.

Men must realize that they can meet their needs for power and intimacy, not through their appearance but through their personal skills. They must cultivate the skills of expressing warmth, intimacy, sensitivity, and caring. Many men eventually turn to these emotional ways of relating as opposed to the more physical ways. It helps to have a friend to talk to about this issue. When a man sees a friend losing his hair without being too upset, it sets an example to be followed. Group counseling also works for men with this concern and also for the decline in sexual performance that many middle adulthood men experience.

Sexual performance

A decline in sexual performance is the most distressing physical "ailment" of men in the later part of middle adulthood, in my opinion. This problem refers to the longer amount of time that it takes to achieve an erection, periodic failure to gain or maintain an erection, and the longer time that it takes to regain an erection after having ejaculated. All of these changes in a man's performance have a physical component in that all muscle tissue is not as effective as it was years earlier and that lack of appropriate exercise affects all body parts. The physically and sexually active man will maintain a certain degree of sexual competence, but the psychological factor is of even greater importance for most men, I believe.

In the specific case of not achieving an erection or losing an erection, the answer in many cases is psychological rather than physical. The primary reason why men don't perform sexually, in my experience, is the reason why people don't perform well at anything, which is anxiety caused by stress. Men always wonder, "Why does stress choose to affect my sexual performance and not other areas of my life?"

First, stress does affect other areas of a man's life, but when he has a sexual performance problem then all else goes unnoticed. Also, stress has had a slow effect on other areas so that a decline in work productivity, for example, has been less evident than failure to achieve or maintain an erection that often takes place quite suddenly and is impossible to deny.

Secondly, I believe that stress affects the area of men's lives where they have the biggest ego investment. That is, stress hits men hardest at the point where they satisfy a lot of their power needs. Consequently, sexual performance may be most vulnerable to stress for many men.

One man was relatively concerned about his career, friends, and family, but was very concerned about his appearance and his sexual performance. When he began to lose his hair and wrinkles emerged rather suddenly, he started to have periodic impotence. Over time, he began to gain some confidence in himself that was not related to physical attractiveness or sexual ability but more to how he related to other people. As these relationships strengthened, he regained his sexual performance.

Sexual dysfunction is an emotional trauma, and men want a quick cure. Viagra may provide that quick cure, but I would like to spend more time in counseling men who use this medication to determine the psychological impact of its use. The other cure, in my opinion, is a change in lifestyle to one that has less stress and a change in the relationship with one's sexual partner.

When the children leave the nest

Fathers, even divorced fathers who are emotionally intimate with their kids, have a very difficult time when their children leave home for college, marriage, the service, or a job. Many men don't realize how invested they are until after their children leave. Some men feel depressed and lonely, but don't know why until they examine and identify their relationships with their children.

One man said, "I don't know what to do anymore. I spent so much time at my son's athletic events that I didn't have time for any interests of my own. I don't even have any interests really." This man is in for a difficult adjustment period. It's similar to grieving after the death of a loved one. Some men try to hang on to the child. Others withdraw and exclude themselves from contact with the child. Both of these strategies will fail to make them feel better.

When a child leaves home, I recommend that men review the good memories of the child and add to them the events that are happening now to the child. One father drove from Philadelphia to Manhattan to have dinner with his daughter who recently moved there, even though it's a two-hour (or more) ride each way in rush hour traffic. There was no special occasion; just a dinner for the two of them. No amount of time and distance is likely to separate these two.

After the children leave, fathers should invite children to be as much a part of their lives as the children can manage. By making their needs clear, men can increase the chance that those needs will be met. However, men should not resort to bargaining with children in order to get him or her to stay emotionally close or physically close. I remember a heavily-invested father who tried to lure his son into attending college near home by offering an apartment and a new car. This father should beware of a backlash from his son who, if he stayed in the area, may later regret doing so and wish that he had gone away to college. Regret could become resentment toward the father.

When children leave the nest, even the most stable and well-adjusted family is disrupted. Marital relationships that appear solid sometimes dissolve, and break-ups are high during middle adulthood.

The Social Scene

The social life of the man in the later stage of middle adulthood depends primarily on his marital status. Married men have social lives that involve their wives. Men who are "single"; that is, divorced, widowed or never-married have a very different experience trying to meet their needs for intimacy.

Divorced or widowed

The divorced or widowed man in the later stage of middle adulthood who had been married for a long time prior to his single status may be highly emotionally disrupted. His long marriage probably established a familiar social role that no longer remains. He may have children to care for and a home too. This usually means doing chores that he's never had to do before, but his biggest problem is loneliness. Men who never thought much about their feelings now struggle with a sense of longing for social contact that sometimes can be overwhelming. These men took for granted that these needs were met while married. Men who seem to be so independent often realize that they became dependent to some degree during their married years, and now the person on whom they depended is gone.

One way that many men handle the loneliness is to remarry soon after they have been divorced or widowed. I believe that some studies show that men who have been divorced or widowed after a lengthy relationship are likely to remarry within a year after the end of that relationship. Unfortunately, these men often make inappropriate choices that often lead to another divorce.

Some men will never remarry. These men don't want to "start over", as they describe it. The phrase "start over" means to many men that to date and remarry would be the same as dating and marrying when they were in early adulthood. There is some similarity, I believe, but women and men are different at this life stage and so are different in their courtship and in marriage. Divorced and widowed men shouldn't use their fear of "starting over" as a reason for not dating. Perhaps they're concerned about being rejected during the dating process.

Never-married

The man who never married and is now in the later phase of middle adulthood may not have met the right woman or more likely focused his life on the attainment of power rather than intimacy. As he approaches, enters, or ends his forties, he may evaluate his life and find that he's unhappy. The typical man has several reactions at this point in his life. He panics and marries in haste, or he resigns himself to a life without a partner. This is a very vulnerable time for many men.

One man's panic caused a significant awareness as he approached forty. He had been finding fault with every woman he dated because he felt that his father's marriage had kept his father from attaining greater achievements. This man said, "I always saw my father as being trapped in marriage. He could have done so much more, but my mother didn't support or encourage him. She wasn't very ambitious." His fear that he would carry out his father's pattern (or his perception of his father's pattern) kept him from marriage until he finally began to examine his inner fears.

One of the problems of the never-married mid-life man who panics and searches for a wife is that he has little experience at long-term relationships, has a fairly set life-style, and may have unreasonable expectations of a wife. Consequently, this man will have trouble relating to the best of women. Of course, if he can begin to accept that marriage to anyone will permanently alter his entire lifestyle then he may be able to make the necessary changes that will lead to a lasting and satisfying marriage. A man who doesn't intend to change as much as is necessary for a marriage to survive is in for a shock.

Another problem for the never-married man is that his prospective wife may have children by a previous marriage. Marriage is a major change, but an instant family where the children are not biologically his own is another matter. Many men balk at marrying a woman with children. Raising children isn't easy, and the never-married man has no experience with this task. Perhaps he has a macho feeling of not wanting to care for another man's offspring. Never-married men often avoid women with children, except for a few men who look on an "instant family" as a way to make up for "lost time." They want a family, and a woman with children is the answer for them.

A similar issue is the potential wife who has no children but wants to have children. Similarly, there's the woman who can no longer bear children herself but wants to adopt a child. The expectations of these women may be more than the mid-life man bargained for. One man might decline to marry her and later feels guilty because he doesn't want children. Another man might marry her and later regret that he has children to raise whom he didn't want. Some men feel trapped and resentful that they are not wanted just for themselves instead of as potential fathers. In other words "Does she want to marry me for me or as a way to have children?" If men could work through these feelings they may be able to work out a compromise that would allow a marriage to occur.

However, some never-married men seek marriage at this life stage primarily in order to have children. They may not admit it, but they want heirs to succeed them. The whole idea concerns mortality. A way (maybe the only way) to get close to being immortal is through heritage. Leaving children behind is a sign that a man was really here on earth, as so many achievements are forgotten after death. To a man who had a fantasy of making a lasting impression, perhaps through his work, having heirs may be his last and only chance to "leave his mark." Marrying in order to have children is probably a thought of all of men, but it should not be the only reason.

Some men don't panic and decide that they will be fine without being married because the right woman hasn't come along. These men must deal with the fears of every man who is at this juncture of his life, and they must face them without a partner. If they feel strong enough to face these fears then they may do well being single. They will have to do some things to make sure that their life is both satisfying and meaningful.

Guidelines for the never-married man

The first and most important thing for the never-married man (or any single man, perhaps) is to establish a group of friends on whom he can rely no matter what the situation demands. He should be able not only to socialize with them but also to receive help from them in the day-to-day ways that can strain the bonds of friendship. One single man reported that a friend of his would help him work on his house, listen to him talk about his career without advice, and allow him to feel unguarded and vulnerable. That's the kind of friend a man needs.

Incidentally, single men should have friendships with married people, women and men, old and young, as well as other single men. A variety of friends will be more stimulating and ultimately more satisfying than a group of single men only.

The next step, in order of importance, is to establish a routine and stick to it. At work the routine may be established by the boss; but, for example, men should set a pattern of going out to some of the same places for lunch and sometimes to a new place. They should meet the people who work there and who own the place. They should always take a vacation and consider taking it in the same place each year if it's a place where familiar faces return each year. The idea is that a man can set a routine that keeps him from sliding into a boring rut. This rut can happen to all men if they aren't aware of how easily their momentum can diminish.

The next step for single men is to join a community service project that helps other people in the neighborhood. This activity will give a man a sense of significance or importance that will not come through recreation or work. The feeling is also referred to as a sense of meaning or purpose in life.

In leisure activity, single men should participate in seasonal sports: ski in the winter, play golf in the summer, and get time outside as much as possible. Also, plan regular times for hobbies, such as playing guitar each night or listening to music. In addition, buy season tickets to events from concerts and theatre to athletic events.

One final suggestion is to buy a house and a pet. The home will add to a sense of permanence and also provide an outlet for creative expression through decorating as well as space for entertaining. A house also will provide economic security and demand upkeep that will encourage the development of new skills. The pet will offer companionship and reduce the sense of loneliness.

Chapter Ten

As the World Changes

Marriage Maintenance

After a man has managed to strike a balance between meeting his need for power and his need for intimacy, he faces the challenge of maintaining that balance. Somehow, men don't understand that it takes constant work to meet one's needs both at work and at home.

A job or a marriage could lapse into a rut; consequently, a man feels less powerful and less intimate than ever before. He must find new ways to replenish his feelings of power and intimacy. The primary sources of renewal for the married man with a family are his peer group at work, other couples, and his children.

Peers at work

Peers at work make up the primary social circle for some men. However, peers are acceptable as friends and sources of intimacy only if they are not seen as competitors for rewards. Consequently, certain men have more of an opportunity for friends at work than others do. In occupations where rewards are given according to longevity of service rather than merit, friendships among workers may develop. Historically, these occupations are ones where labor unions are strong and the guidelines for performance are very specific.

However, in white-collar occupations such as business and even in professions such as law and medicine, competition is fierce. Consequently, many men do not open up to their peers for fear of giving away an advantage that may be used against them. Men in these occupations may not actually be in such a head-to-head contest, but it feels that way, and so men remain on guard. When men are on guard, the opportunity for intimacy disappears.

Even in occupations where competition is present, men can establish friendships if they are willing to spend time working on them. It takes time to have lunch with someone or to meet after work. Once a man has taken the time, he must take the risk to either ask for feedback or self-disclose something personal about himself.

Requesting feedback puts a man in a vulnerable spot where he asks this potential friend to tell him his honest opinion about a topic of importance. It's a question such as, "How do you think that I'm perceived by the boss or by other people here at work?" or "What do you think of that big project I just finished?" He may not receive a totally honest answer, but instead a socially appropriate one, such as, "You're doing great! Everyone thinks well of you," but it's a start. It takes a while for people to believe that a man who asks for honest feedback actually wants to hear it.

In addition men may choose to self-disclose some personal thoughts or feelings to a peer to see if he (or she) will respond with genuine concern. Men could reveal some feeling about a family member, a physical ailment, or a worry about the future economic picture. For example, three men friends were chatting when one of them blurted out that he was concerned about the size of the scar that had formed after he'd had surgery for a vasectomy. The other two revealed that they also had vasectomies and began to describe how they felt about it. It seemed to open up their friendship to a more intimate level.

One final observation is that relationships in the work place often do not extend homeward. Many men have friends at work but do nothing with them in the evenings or on weekends. One man revealed that he tried to socialize with a friend from work and found that the friend could talk only about work activities and not his feelings about them. Some men aren't willing to take the risk that they and their friend from work will be able to have a more in-depth relationship. Other men sense that they will not have much to discuss once they exhaust work-related topics. Other men don't want to take away the time from activities with their family.

Peers at work are a great opportunity for friendships because men have so many common experiences with each other there. Expanding their relationships outside of work might not be successful, but they'll never know unless they try. If intimacy with peers at work is unsuccessful, then men can try other sources such as civic, religious, or community groups.

Couples

It seems that married mid-life men conduct almost all of their social activities among other married couples. However, when a married man makes friends as a couple, it's different than when he makes friends by himself. When two people meet, they have to decide if they like each other enough to have a friendship. When four people meet, all four have to agree if the friendship is going to develop. Many men have told me of meeting and liking a couple (or one of the couple) while his wife did not like either of them. Or a man met a couple and liked the man but not the woman. Meanwhile, his wife liked the woman but not the man. In both situations it's unlikely that a friendship will develop among any of them.

Some married men interact periodically with other men, usually playing sports or attending a sporting event, but not much else and not very often. However, married men in other areas of the world, such as Ireland, Australia, Latin America and Scandinavia spend time with other men at taverns or private clubs talking about events of the day.

One theory or bit of folklore about married men without men friends is that these men want to enhance their marriage, and so they spend their free time with their spouse. This doesn't seem accurate to me. I suspect that married men without men friends probably spend the same amount of time with their spouse as men who have men friends. Furthermore, I think that married men would have a better marriage if they would spend more time with men friends. Men who feel reinforced and reassured by intimate friendships with other men may maintain better relationships with their wives.

Another theory is that after years of marriage men are insecure with people other than their spouse. Dependency develops in which men become less comfortable in social situations with anyone other than their wives. There may be some validity to this theory. Many men say that they don't feel "right" when they go out by themselves or with a male friend instead of their spouse.

No matter why married mid-life men have few friends, there is a middle ground where a man can have a solid relationship with his wife and have friendships with men. Men could start by re-establishing relationships with former friends.

Some men hang on to friends from high school, college, or the military service as if they know that these friends will be important in later years. These men keep friends from the period that was most significant in their personal development, I believe. If high school was most important then they'll maintain friendships from high school. If buddies from the military service were important then these are the friendships that will be maintained.

A man recalled, "I really had to work to keep up with my friends from high school when I was working out of state. Thank God for, no, thank the Smith Company for having an email account that I could use to keep in touch with my friends back in Philadelphia."

The best rule of thumb, in my opinion, is that a man can't have too many friends. A man must realize that it takes time to develop friendships and energy to maintain them. Friends contribute to the stability of a marriage and the likelihood that it will endure.

Children

The activities of a man's children can shape his social life, which may be good or bad. A man could spend his free time going to practices or rehearsals, raising funds for the school, attending games or performances, and talking with other parents at events or at the end-of-the-season banquet. One good aspect about planning a social life around his kids' activities is it leaves a man very few choices to make. His kids' social life determines his own social schedule and guarantees that he will have something to do with little effort in planning it. It's no wonder that so many men feel lonely when their children move away from home.

Involving himself with only a child's activities is not a good idea because a man spends too much time in the parent role. This results in his having fewer opportunities for intimacy with his wife. A man and wife need to interact with each other some time as husband and wife, dating partners, lovers, and friends which doesn't happen very often when the main reason for being together is their child.

Interacting with children can be a source of intimacy for some men. One man, who made the father role primary in his life, became more open to expressing his feelings, but only to his children. His children demanded and provoked him so much that the feelings ranging from rage to joy could not be denied. His wife saw this opening and moved in. She asked for him to relate to her in this more open and more compassionate way. She said to him, "You're more affectionate and open toward the children than you are to me. Why don't you talk to me the way that you talk to them?" She also observed, "You always get in a better mood when you're around the children. I wish that I could get you in a good mood the way they do." These statements depict a man who is able to let down his defenses with his children but not with his wife. He shuts out his wife, except for her role as a co-parent, in an effort to resist her attempts at intimacy. Hopefully this man, and others like him, learns to relate as openly with his wife as with his children.

In my work with couples, I've seen that it's safer for many men to interact with their spouse in the role of co-parent because the focus can be on the children and not on themselves. It's a diversion tactic. I recommend that these couples spend time doing couple activities even though it may reduce the time they spend with their children.

Overall, married men have lots of opportunities for social interaction. This social interaction usually leads to the developing of acquaintances rather than friends, which precludes intimacy, but this can change at any time. A man's participation in some or all of these social situations will have an impact on his relationship with his wife. A man who is highly involved with friends may be spending too little time with his wife, and so his marriage may suffer. On the other hand, a man who spends little or no time with friends may feel unfulfilled, thus his marriage may suffer. It's important to have several sources by which a man can meet his needs for intimacy.

Reasons for Marital Break-up in Middle Adulthood

I believe that the reasons for marital break-up initiated by men in the latter part of middle adulthood are based on their feeling a loss of power and having too little intimacy. The key factor in weathering this loss is a man's reserve strength; that is, how resilient is he at recovering from a major drain on his resources?

Work

Either a stoppage or a plateau at work can trigger a man's anxiety and lead to a marital break-up. Some men are fired or demoted. Others reach a plateau where it is clear that they will progress no further. Although being fired is probably the most stressful in the short run, it may be the best situation in the long run. When a man is fired due to a company take-over or reorganization, there is a sudden shock but one that is clear and definitive. Consequently, he can make plans for another job or, in some cases, another career. On the other hand, when he realizes that he's on a plateau, he feels depressed.

In both of these situations men feel powerless, worthless, and angry. Many men take out their feelings on their wives in a direct and antagonistic way, thus leading to a break-up. Other men turn their feelings inward and create a wall between themselves and their spouse that eventually leads one of them to leave. Only the strongest marriages survive. If men can identify and cope with their feelings directly then they may be able to continue their marriage.

Physical ailments

The onset of physical problems points to a man's frailty and vulnerability. At mid-life he cannot avoid these aches as he did when he was younger. Now the physical ailments don't go away.

Physical ailments also affect a man's reliance upon his wife, and so he realizes several things. One is that he is dependent on her for some degree of nursing care. Therefore, he thinks his role of protector and provider is challenged in his own eyes and in the eyes of his spouse. It's a frightening and painful time when a man who has proclaimed for decades, "I can take care of myself and the family too, so don't try to help me," now has to admit a weakness and allow others to care for him.

In addition, there are other physical changes related to aging. The loss of hair, the decline of one's physique due to excess weight, sagging skin, or anything that is outwardly noticeable is a big blow to a man's sense of power. The loss of his physical attractiveness is directly related to his feeling of sexual attractiveness; that is, if a man feels physically attractive to his wife, or to women in general, then he feels confident in his ability to keep a woman near to him.

It's crucial for men to learn that they are worthwhile people even if they're not perfect physical specimens. Sometimes a man refuses to accept his physical decline. He may attempt to re-capture his youthful appearance. Re-capture usually means buying new and fashionable clothing typically worn by a man several decades younger, joining a health club, dying his hair (or having a transplant), buying a sporty car or flirting with attractive women. This reaction provides only a temporary relief from the reality of aging.

Sometimes a man divorces his wife because he fears she will leave him if he becomes less powerful (meaning less youthful). In other words, he decides to divorce her before she can divorce him. Of course, the wife has no idea as to what's going on. It will take a lot of reassurance by his wife to convince this frightened man that he can appear less youthful and still be acceptable to her.

Sexual decline

Closely related to physical ailments of aging is the decline in sexual prowess, which also causes a man either to cling to his wife or to leave her. The decline in sexual performance is usually seen by a slower initial arousal, a decline in the overall firmness of the penis when aroused, difficulty in maintaining an erection during lovemaking, and slower arousal after having ejaculated. These changes are very disappointing to most men.

Some men seem to accept these changes by saying that it's a natural part of their overall physical decline. It's not pleasant, they say, but it's not the end of their lives. Other men feel cheated and depressed. These men say, in essence, "I can't make love like I used to do, and so making love isn't enjoyable anymore." This can lead to passive resentment and bitterness resulting in withdrawal from sexual activity entirely.

Men who are more prone to act out may blame their wives for not arousing them as much as they used to do. In these cases some men push the wife to new sexual practices, pornographic movies, or provocative lingerie. This may have some initial impact, but I believe that it's only a temporary solution. Men must deal with the issue that scares them so much; that is, the fear that they will lose power in their marital relationship. It's unfortunate that these men think that women will leave them because of a decline in sexual performance. Most women are willing, in my counseling practice, to work to allay their husband's concerns about sexual performance and their overall relationship. Of course, the use of prescription medications for erectile dysfunction has been the answer for many men and had been very helpful in restoring their functioning. Not all men will seek this solution due to embarrassment.

Still other men seek out another woman to see if sex is better with someone else. Many men become highly aroused with another woman, which proves to them that their sexual decline is the fault of their wives. Consequently, they may divorce or separate from her. Sadly, their problems will return in time as the "newness" of the other woman diminishes. The excitement of a new person is enough to arouse most any man, but it doesn't mean that the new woman is inherently better than his current wife. It only means that she's new. Hopefully, men will realize that it's not the woman they're with but the issue in their heads that is the problem. Men who leave their wives to "date" other women (which really means have sex with other women) usually return within three months in my informal observations. However, they don't come back if they have formed an emotional attachment to another woman who fills an intimacy void that had developed between the man and his wife.

Boredom

Boredom hits men and women hard if they have been married for at least fifteen years, have adolescent children, and are in a stable lifestyle (job, home, parents, friends). Boredom is a condition of men feeling less powerful and less intimate with their spouse. This occurs because their relationship has become emotionally repressed or restricted, open communication has stopped, or has become distracted by outside interests and has become predictable. This condition is accompanied by a decline in interest in one's spouse.

As a couple lives together over a period of years they adapt to the idiosyncrasies of each other in order to keep from becoming depressed or angry with each other. This functional adaptation or tolerance is fine, except that in order to carry it out a man suppresses most of his entire realm of feelings. As he covers up his uncomfortable feelings, he also buries his more pleasant ones.

Adolescent kids take a lot of attention away from the marital relationship, which contributes to a distance between husband and wife. Coming together as parents doesn't necessarily contribute to a marital relationship.

A stable life style, although generally quite preferable to recurrent crises or tragedies, allows many men to become complacent and take their marriage for granted. Taking a marriage for granted means that a man wants to have the good parts of the relationship to last forever without doing much to maintain that current level of functioning. He doesn't dislike his wife. He just wants to stop working at the relationship.

Consequently, men don't try as hard to listen, to care for, or to support the woman whom they first thought was so special. It takes a tremendous amount of time and energy to maintain a relationship, which many men don't seem to realize. They apparently believe that relationships operate on inertia or some other strange force. It doesn't work that way.

Many men assume that their relationship will be maintained by sporadic efforts such as dinner out on their wives's birthday and a vacation once a year (with the children). Relationships need frequent and regular communication and demonstration of a man's interest in and concern for his partner.

But how can men realize that they're bored if men are so unaware of their feelings? Unfortunately, it usually takes a shock to wake them up. The shock typically comes when the wife has an affair (or close encounter) or even when the man has an affair (or close encounter). Most affairs have the effect of jolting a couple into doing something that should have been done earlier in a less dramatic and traumatic way, but they were not able to do so. People enter affairs because they feel lonely, powerless, and detached (no intimacy), which is part of the boredom, and then realize how badly they really had been feeling as the affair progresses.

Although an affair by either husband or wife can shock the both of them into recognizing the boredom and motivating them to eliminate it, an affair by a wife is different than an affair by a husband, I believe. When a wife has an affair and her husband finds out (regardless of whether she tells him or he stumbles on to it), he has a tougher time getting over it and rebuilding the relationship than if he has an affair and his wife finds out about it. There are several issues here.

When a man discovers his wife's affair, he's angry and upset but also is worried that he can never regain his wife as solely "his own". Consequently, he may divorce her and seek a new partner. When a woman discovers a man's outside relationship, she's hurt but sees it as his needing sexual validation or as an attempt to regain his adolescence. Therefore, she waits and helps him return to her after this brief period of insanity. It's as if he was never really hers in the exclusive sense that she was for him.

However, men can beat the boredom and restore intimacy by less painful means than by having an affair. The following guidelines may be useful.

Initiate! No matter what it is, any man's wife will appreciate the thought. She may be disappointed and somewhat amazed that by now he still doesn't know her favorite flower, but those feelings will pass quickly in the face of a thoughtful bouquet of any type for no apparent reason. Initiation of any activity or thoughtfulness must be in addition to the regular recognition of her birthday, anniversary, and Valentine's Day, which are an absolute necessity to celebrate. A man should give gifts for no apparent reason, do favors for her that he knows she will like, or take over a household chore so she can have some free time to herself. The gift of time may be the best gift anyone can ever give.

Spend more time away from home. By traveling, sightseeing, or walking around the block it's possible to vary the daily routine and so to break the deadening pattern of social roles. It's easier to revive the roles of spouse, friend, and lover when away from the reminders present in the home. However, don't make the mistake of relying on "the big vacation" to beat the boredom. The impact of these vacations fades quickly. A better plan is to take shorter and more frequent mini-vacations, such as a weekend every several months. Once-a-year vacations fade quickly, but mini-vacations fight the boredom year round, such as one couple who celebrate "month-a-versaries" of their wedding.

Buy something. A man attempting to get out of boredom should acquire something new for himself, for his spouse or for the house. The key word is new. Buying something for the house is good because it's an investment in which the couple can both share. Shopping together for a household item also gets a couple out together. Such shopping should be for decorative items rather than major purchases such as a refrigerator or a sofa. The big items often stir up anxiety due to their high price or the practical issues such as, "Will it last?", "What features does it have?", or "Does it fit into the space in our home?" When shopping, either alone or with their wives, men should never ask, "Where will we put it?"

Turn off the television. This allows a couple to spend more time talking with each other. Designate one half-hour each day or evening in which both partners agree to talk about topics other than the house or the kids. The designated time shuts out other obligations and interruptions. Some couples think of it as having company. Don't take phone calls. The avoidance of the kids and the house as topics for discussion during this half-hour means that the couple will be more likely to talk about self-oriented topics such as work or friends or even current events. The idea is to move the couple closer to each other emotionally by talking about topics that are more intimate. This may sound simple to accomplish, but most couples in my experience find it very difficult to accomplish.

Do something together. In addition to their half-hour together, the couple should share some recreation time by playing cards or a board game. In this way a couple can increase their interaction slowly and without talking too much.

Have a party. Start big by inviting everyone or start small by having one couple or even one single person. In this way a couple can generate some excitement in the social area that may extend into their personal relationship.

Touch her. Couples who are bored rarely touch. One result of pulling away from each other emotionally is a lack of physical contact. In order to break through this barrier men should touch their wives several times each day, not counting the obligatory goodbye kiss on the way out the door in the morning. If there's no goodbye kiss then start giving one. Add a hello kiss at the end of the day. And one at bedtime. And one in the morning upon waking. This recommendation is contrived, but an increase in touching may allow the wife to be more responsive to verbal messages that the man gives.

What's Love Have To Do With It?

Love is best discussed in terms of specific behavior that may indicate the presence or absence of love. Love, in my opinion, is a very general emotional state of arousal during which time people do things for each other that they wouldn't do ordinarily. While women often ask the "Do you really love me?" question in order to gain reassurance, men are best approached by discussing overt behavior. With couples with whom I work, I discuss love in terms of passion, commitment, and intimacy. If passion, commitment, and intimacy are present in a couple's relationship then love exists. However, men and women seem to rank these qualities in a different order of importance.

When men and women marry, they often both have passion at the top of their list. However, men and women change after the honeymoon, and then friction starts. Married men and women soon find their order of priorities of love to be:

Men's Priorities:	Women's Priorities:
1) Commitment	1) Intimacy
2) Passion & Intimacy	2) Passion
	3) Commitment

Men's commitment grows slowly and overtakes first place as passion declines. This leaves passion and intimacy tied for last place. Meanwhile, the wife has felt her passion slip, but intimacy remains very high and maybe rises even higher on the list than passion at the time she married. However, commitment is not high as long as she is deciding if intimacy and passion can be regained with this man she married.

Of course, passion fades for both men and women as they become more distracted by work, family, and home. Some writers say that as passion fades, commitment grows. A different view is that men develop commitment after they have suffered the agony of realizing that they are frail and vulnerable, thus needing the stability and care of a partner. Perhaps both views are true.

Commitment is shown by the man who said, "I'm staying because I know that life is never easy. So, I've stopped looking for the perfect woman, job, or money that will make life easy. There's just not any payoff for the stuff I'd been searching for. I'd been searching for the wrong things. But it's not too late! I'm trying to slow down and see people as people and not ignore them. That means my wife, my kids, and the people I work with. It's more important now to have the feelings of satisfaction of being with them then doing the other things I'd been doing."

Much of what men learned about love came from their fathers, I believe. First and foremost, they learned to keep almost all feelings inside of themselves, especially feelings that portray them as vulnerable, such as love. Tenderness is the worst feeling to show.

Fathers also taught their sons how to be loyal and honest and committed to a struggle that wasn't going to be easy. Fathers taught sons, by example, that women are hard to deal with because they get upset (angry, disappointed, worried, etc.), and there's little to do except to wait it out until it passes. They can try to stop her from being upset, but that usually makes things worse and is a sign of not being very smart. The result is to be calm, aloof, and conciliatory. This model doesn't work well today, I believe.

Too much has changed in the world so that men cannot afford to use the defense of stoic denial of their feelings and withdrawal from their wives. The demands of the current decades force men to be disloyal to the model set forth by their fathers and to try out a new model. A man feels disloyal when he does something that differs from that which he saw his father demonstrate. Nevertheless, men must stop waiting it out as their fathers did. They must move into the emotional arena and hope that they can be loyal to their fathers in other ways that are more important. For more on this topic read, *Finding Our Fathers: The Unfinished Business of Manhood* by Samuel Osherson.

Men and women who seek to understand men will eventually learn that love is not the answer, but is the result of working to gain intimacy in a world that holds out power as the answer. A useful read on this topic is *I Only Say This Because I Love You* by Deborah Tannen, which I recommend to many couples in counseling.

Chapter Eleven

Balancing Power and Intimacy

There are no simple lessons or cookbook steps to follow in order to achieve a power-intimacy balance. For most men, the playing field is filled with rules that make it difficult. To achieve a balance, one must give up playing the traditional game that men are told to play in our Western culture. I've used the sports metaphor with many, probably most, of my men clients. I've said, "You've got to get out of that game. You're killing yourself. It's a game no man can win." But it's very difficult to leave the game because men think it's the only game that exists. I try to show them that there are other games.

Another metaphor I use is one of multiple pathways to travel from one point to another. I try to convince men that they don't have to travel the accepted path to meet their needs. Just because we are told that a particular path is acceptable for men to follow doesn't mean that the path is the right one for us. We must search for the path that is the right one for each of us.

How do we make such a paradigm shift or change in approach to living? It's a difficult process and usually involves dealing with anxiety. Psychologists and counselors have long examined anticipatory anxiety, sometimes termed "stage-fright." It's the gnawing feeling in the pit of your stomach when you are about to do something in which you might not be successful. Sometimes it can be debilitating. Sometimes it can be motivating.

Living with Anxiety

Debilitating anxiety needs special attention and professional help. When most men experience this anxiety about seeking new sources of power, different types of power, or of seeking intimacy, they are inhibited rather than debilitated. This inhibition causes them to return to their familiar and comfortable routine. It's why people sit in the same pews in church. It's why men eat lunch alone. Familiar patterns calm anxiety but don't gain power or intimacy.

Because the anxiety is based on one's anticipation of an upcoming event or encounter, the anxiety can be managed or reduced. When the event or encounter is known ahead of time, it can't sneak up on you. The problem is that men have so many and such well-defined patterns of avoiding the anxiety; i.e., rituals or comforting patterns, that they engage them automatically without being aware of the anticipatory anxiety or their avoidance response to it. Thus the first step for a man is to become aware of his own anxiety and that he's handling it in a way that avoids it rather than views it as a barrier to his success and confronts it. Please note that it's easy for most men to recognize their anxiety when they face the major life steps, such as job changes, marriage, and having children. It's much more difficult and important to recognize the anxiety that guides the seemingly small and unimportant steps such as looking for a job, asking someone for a date, and having sex.

Gaining awareness of anxiety over daily decisions is difficult without help. Most men can't step back and look at their day-to-day behavior and question themselves. The best help I know of is that of a friend or mentor. The right friend or mentor can pose the difficult question of "What makes you always...?" This question forces a man to focus on why he acts the way that he does. Most men will answer superficially, "Because I'm comfortable doing it." The second question should be, "What are you avoiding by doing it?" For a few men the real answer is "failure"; failure at achieving power and/or intimacy. After an initial denial, some amount of discussion could lead to better ways of coping with the anxiety and to reduce this barrier to change.

The many effective strategies of coping with anxiety are well described in self-help books everywhere. I often recommend and give out, *Feeling Good* by David Burns. Depending on how much awareness men have gained, I may also recommend *The Road Less Traveled* by M. Scott Peck. Biography can also be helpful to give men role models for struggling with life. I especially like *A Pirate Looks at Fifty* by Jimmy Buffett. For most men, I'm less interested in teaching the skills of coping with anxiety than in helping them to allow themselves to be aware each day that anxiety is inevitable. It's something to accept and face directly, but not to conquer.

Accepting life as full of ongoing anxiety can lead some men to depression and rage as I described in chapter two, while others see it as a challenge or an opportunity to better themselves or at least to test themselves. Viewing the daily anxiety of life as a challenge, test or opportunity means seeing the world as a very different game or path than the one posed so dominantly in our society today. This is a different interpretation because the man measures his success or failure in terms of how well he honestly tries. Effort becomes the yardstick instead of the usual measures of money, status, possessions and people; e.g., wife and children.

Viewing life as a journey rather than a destination makes a huge difference in living one's life. In a life where the man's game is to grow and learn about himself, for example, anxiety is a motivator to learn more. Anxiety to this man is not to be avoided or denied. It is a source of feedback and nothing is more terrifying than that.

Moving into this new game of testing and growth without adding up the score of one's bank account or social events in a datebook really alters one's thinking. A man must begin to believe that he will feel powerful and intimate with others by his new behavior. He just may not ever achieve the symbols that his society tells him are important, and he must accept that possibility. However, he will not be alone.

I believe that as men challenge themselves to face their anxieties, other people will view them quite differently. Some will be attracted to this new man and others won't. Others notice changes in behavior, and these men will gain new and different relationships as they change. As men become less competitive, aggressive, and emotionally restricted, their new behavior will be admired, respected and approached by people who value this kind of man. Although the transition to the new game may take a long time and may be lonely, it is likely to reap rewards.

The lonely aspect of the journey or new path is something that many men find most disturbing. Existential writers have told us that we are all essentially alone in this world and most men, probably unconsciously, react by building social networks that work to reduce their feelings of being alone. These systems work only to a certain degree. Late at night or at other times, men's awareness of their mortality and lack of ultimate power in the universe tends to be terrifying. Each man must come to terms with being alone, regardless of how many people he gathers around him. Coming to the sense of peace that accompanies his accommodation will allow him to move on this new path more quickly. The new game will seem less forced upon him but instead, a decision he made willingly.

If a man accepts that his personal growth is a new game or path to be traveled, and his efforts are important in and of themselves, what about finding a direction on which these efforts can be focused? Gerry Spence, the Wyoming attorney and author, wrote about his path in *How to Argue and Win Every Time*. Some people, like Spence, believe that we live best when we try to do the right thing, no matter how difficult it is to find it and no matter if our efforts are recognized by the mainstream markers of our society. Doing the right thing may be acting in ways that are unselfish, non-critical, cooperative, giving, helpful, and comforting. And many times the game is recognized on the scoreboard that most men use in our society.

The Forces Men Face

One force men face is measuring up to the visible criteria for manhood established by our Western society; e.g., money, zip code, job title. The suggestion I make to men is to become less visible. In other words use the invisible markers such as efforts in doing the right thing, making others' lives more bearable, adherence to principles, openness, honesty, and loyalty.

Another way to think of this new game is to become more anonymous. Men are pressured daily to "make a name for themselves" or to "make a mark." I believe that gaining recognition in the traditional visible way distances men from other people by making these potential friends into fellow competitors, thus reducing the chance for intimacy.

I suggest to men that they lower their profiles by, for example, recognizing the work of others. Although this strategy of teamwork and team leadership would not be rewarded in some careers or specific companies, this behavior would be greatly valued by others. "Working behind the scenes" is helpful to any organization and establishes a man as someone less to be feared or envied and as less of a competitor.

Competition is a major force that men face. They have been trained for it throughout their lives. I suggest that in this new game men become cooperative instead of competitive. Again, in some organizations competition and the typical win-lose system will be used to reward and punish men, but not in all of them. By becoming cooperative, men become less threatening to each other. When they become less threatening, they become more approachable to others and others become more receptive to their approaches. Approaching others is the first step toward gaining intimacy.

Furthermore, formation of personal alliances can be truly rewarding as long as both persons are open about their agendas. As personal bonds are strengthened, the power of influencing others increases. The main agenda should be the achievement of intimacy. I suggest to men that they work to form relationships whose only agenda would be to assist other people in the achievement of their goals, a very selfless venture. Paradoxically, when we assist others without asking for a favor in return, we increase the influence we have over others in a new and enjoyable way. I know a graphic designer of websites and other electronic media, who works for a very competitive public relations company, who also assists local graphic artists and painters to show their works at various venues. He helps his own competition.

Life Themes

Many men find slogans or themes helpful to ground them in seeking a new path or getting out of the old game and into a new one. Although it may sound trivial or childish, we all need to be reminded of what to do, because it's very easy to fall back into our old habits. And we'll be playing a new game in a world in which almost everyone else is playing the old one. At the risk of seeming trivial or sounding like a self-help meeting, let me share several slogans that I prefer to call life themes.

One is: It's not a race; it's a journey. As I've explained, the shift is to experiencing rather than trying to gain a prize. I've had many men in my office who have told me of their "race" and how unhappy they are despite their "winnings."

Another is: There's enough for everyone. The life message here is that there's not a finite number of prizes, so don't act like there are.

An additional one is: Do the right thing. This one is difficult, because men have trouble recognizing the right thing. One senior level manager always tells others in his organization, "Never lie." He reports that people find it very difficult not to embellish their accomplishments and avoid mentioning their failures.

One further theme is: Help just one person. This theme was told to me many years ago by a man who taught in a high school and went way beyond just one person, but found that the theme was manageable when it was just one in number.

Another powerful theme is: We're all on the same team. This one implies that despite how we are told that we are different by our employers and by divisive world leaders, we are human beings who can meet our needs by cooperating. Of course, there are obvious differences among us such as race, socioeconomic status and access to basic survival needs, but we all want the same things.

An often-trivialized theme is: Be in the moment. It suggests that we reduce our forward-looking planning or our backward-looking analysis and see how we feel right now, both physically and emotionally. This theme is dangerously close to the clichéd, "Stop and smell the flowers." Sadly, we need to focus on the moment a lot in order to gain a new source of information to guide us. I remember a group of people who emerged from a restaurant in the pitch darkness of a small New England town far from the lights of any major city. One man looked up and shared his amazement about the spectacle of all the stars in the clear sky with his companions, all city people who rarely see such a display. Why did this one man, and not the others, notice the heavens? All enjoyed the scene, but one man somehow took notice first. He was in the moment. I sometimes ask men in counseling to keep a record of their daily observations for a week and then ask them to review it with me. I listen for moments in which they have observed their environment and anything about it whether beautiful or ugly, grand or tiny, pleasurable or painful. It's an exercise anyone can do.

A final theme is: If it seems scary, it's probably important. This theme forces men to accept that times when they feel anxious (scared) are probably times that are filled with significant information. The implication is that men should try to determine what makes them nervous and how they can approach the anxiety instead of avoiding it. I ask them to ask themselves, "What's the anxiety telling me?"

Chapter Twelve

Working with Men

In this chapter I have separated suggestions for working with men into a section for counselors and a section for family, friends, and co-workers. However, I believe that all of the suggestions may be used by anyone concerned about the men in their lives, whether the relationship is professional or personal. The first step is engagement, perhaps the most crucial and often mishandled step, and the second is initiation.

For Counselors

Engagement

The initial encounter with men clients or potential clients is very important. I believe that men, and women also, make up their minds instantly if they trust a person who seeks to be their counselor. This does not give a counselor a fair chance to prove himself/herself, but this is reality.

One factor that men use to determine if counseling will work with a particular person is the gender of the counselor. The research suggests that if a man client is allowed to choose a counselor, he will choose a man. I suppose he thinks that a man might understand him. However, some men choose a woman as a counselor because they feel, perhaps unconsciously, that a man counselor might be critical, judgmental or represent a competitor. Once the counseling process begins, it seems that the skill of the counselor becomes the primary factor and the relevance of the gender issue fades quickly. Let me offer some suggestions for both men and women counselors to engage men clients. Men counselors don't automatically know the skills of engagement. Training and supervision are needed.

The first suggestion is to make sure that the client senses that the sessions are private. Privacy of the office and its location make men feel that they won't be observed entering and exiting a place where mental health is discussed. Signs outside the office and waiting rooms with other clients scare men off. I stagger appointments so that clients will not meet each other when entering or leaving the office.

Privacy of phone contact is also important. I ask men whom they have informed about their coming to see me, so I don't call their home or workplace if they prefer me not doing so. I assure them that if I do call their workplace in response to their call or if I need to change an appointment, I won't identify myself (other than my name), and I won't use my title. I have had to deflect several efficient secretaries who have been instructed to find out "the nature of my call" and who I am. I usually say that I'm returning the call and don't know why the call was made to me, even if I'm initiating the call. I tell clients this anecdote. Also I have voice mail on my phones so clients don't have to deal with a secretary, a fact that I tell all of my clients.

I also discuss the insurance and reimbursement issue. Some men worry that someone in the human resource department of their company will see an insurance form and know that they are seeing a psychologist. I ask them to check out this situation with the people in their company who work with insurance and find out some concrete answers about privacy. We rehearse what they can say to the HR person if they wish to do so. I have not had any clients who discovered that privacy was compromised at their workplace, but it makes them feel better to check this out. Of course, I then provide the standard information about confidentiality, exceptions to confidentiality, and HIPAA regulations both verbally and in writing.

As you can see, I start off immediately by addressing concerns that I have found that most men clients have and don't wait for them to emerge from the client. I also frame the concerns and how I have handled them with other clients very concretely. I tell them the issues, and the solutions I've used. Although I tell them that they might not be concerned about this issue, other people with whom I've worked have been concerned about it. Issue first and then solution.

The second major suggestion is to use non-clinical language. Although I have used jargon here such as "counseling", "client", "therapy", "problem", and others, I don't use these terms with men clients unless they use them first and we can agree on what terms we will use in our work together.

Instead of using "counseling" or "therapy" I say, "work together." This reduces the hierarchy between professional and client and makes many men, I believe, more involved. They would like to work with someone but not be "worked on." The concept of "work" is helpful to use, because men want to work not "explore", "discover", "reflect", "gain insight", or even "change."

I don't use the term "clients", but use "people I work with" or "have worked with in the past." Client or patient makes men feel weak or sick, and that will make them drop out. Eventually, some men with whom I've worked for a while refer to themselves as a client or patient and ask me what term they should use. I always say "client" but say that that's a professional bit of jargon.

Furthermore, I don't use "problem" but substitute "issue" or "concern" or "situation." I believe that men want to put their concerns into a context so that they won't be blamed or criticized or held to be fully responsible for where they now find themselves. I can accept that during the engagement process. There's time later to try to fix things, find solutions, and learn about good habits and bad habits. Lastly, instead of "sessions," I use "meetings."

In my opening orientation about procedures; e.g., how long meetings last, payment, gathering address and phone numbers, the privacy issues, etc, I tell the client some information about me. I, of course, give my contact information and so forth, both at the office and at the university where I am employed. Giving my phone number and email address at the university has been important, not only because it gives me credibility, but also because it lets them check me out. Some men look up the faculty in the program where I'm a member, and read about me. More importantly, I tell them how I work and how I view counseling.

An important item I offer is that I've worked with men previously, which is true. Men want that information. I also tell them that I find that men have a tough time now in the current world and I try to help them negotiate the difficulties that they face. I want them to know that I understand the importance of the context in which men operate.

I tell them that I work with most men on a short-term basis, usually less than six months, but that it depends on what issues men present to me. This dispels the fear that they are signing on to an open-ended and never-ending contract. I also tell them that when we finish they can come back at any time in the future because I don't believe in the concept of "cure." I believe that I try to help people get "back on track" or "recuperate" from whatever has been getting to them and that something may get to them in the future. I offer my availability to them without an end point.

As far as problem formation, I say that people have "good habits" and "bad habits", and my job will be to help them identify each group. Then we'll try to change the "bad habits." The concept of both "good" and "bad" habits seeks to show them that they have strengths that I wish to know about and to enhance. Counseling will not just be a deficit-oriented experience. Furthermore, the term, "habits", suggests that people fall into behaviors without much thought and can change with effort. I'm not trying to minimize the pain that men carry to counseling, but I don't want them to think that I will be focused entirely on their feelings. Actually, I probably don't ask about their feelings directly in the first session. It's pretty easy to see and hear how they feel.

After I tell men that I'm a pretty good listener but will make concrete suggestions as I get to know them, I tell them to ask questions at any time during the session about the process. I tell them that the first session is for us to decide if we want to work together. If we don't want to work together, there are lots of other people in the area from which to choose. Hopefully, I can show that he's in charge of the process. A minor point, perhaps, is that I don't take notes in the first session. I may do so in later sessions, but I want to keep the focus securely on him and not my note pad. Moreover, clients wonder what you're writing down about them.

Then I turn it over to the client and ask him to tell me what's been going on lately and what prompted him to make the appointment. I want him to tell his story in his own way, and I say that I will help him do so by asking him to clarify points along the way. I also want to know the particular event or crisis that has triggered his request for counseling. During his description, I try to accurately reflect the content of what he's been saying but not reflect feelings unless he uses a specific feeling word. I ask for concrete examples, such as, "What did you say?" "How long has this been going on?" and "What was your reaction?" I try to get him to be the central figure in the story and not a passive bystander.

Using self-disclosure in the first session is a very powerful tool that may determine if a therapeutic relationship can be formed. I usually don't reveal my personal experience specifically because I believe that clients feel patronized when counselors do this. It can reduce a counselor's credibility among men who want to have an expert work with them. The issue is certainly debatable in the field. I will respond with brief phrases, such as "I understand" or "I know what you're talking about", or "I'm familiar with that situation." I'm hoping to convey that I have some knowledge about his life experiences that may have been acquired in my personal life or through my professional work with men.

Up to this point, I haven't been his pal, but I haven't been too great an authority figure either, I hope. I don't want him to think that I'm his pal because I will lose credibility and power. I don't want him to think of me as an all-knowing authority figure because he will resist that and drop out. It's a tricky balance. A related issue, perhaps, in engaging men clients is that I shake hands with them upon their first entry and often on subsequent meetings and make good eye contact. It's part of how men my age and in my cultural group were raised, I suppose, but I think that it conveys a more personal and egalitarian message.

At the end of the first session, I tell him if I think that I can work with him or not. Sometimes I need to make a referral to someone in a specialty field such as drug and alcohol counseling, for example. I ask him how he thinks the session went and if it was different from what he anticipated. If I decide to work with him, I tell him so, and I tell him that he can think about if he wants to work with me and give me a call with his decision. I say that if he decides not to work with me, I will give him some names and phone numbers of other people. Most times, if I've done a good job, the client will agree immediately to work with me, and I set up a second meeting. Perhaps I might give him a bit of easy homework.

Giving a male client some sort of homework after the first session is a good idea regardless of your theoretical orientation to counseling. First, homework hooks him into coming back the next time to report on what he's done. Of course, if he doesn't do the homework he might not return for the second session in order to avoid being seen as irresponsible or as a failure. I suggest that you make the homework to think about some aspect of what he's described to you in the first session. It's almost impossible for men to not think about what they talked about for an hour with me. Secondly, the homework continues the concrete process of gathering information about the client's situation. Men will see that the process will be about clarity of information, context, and actions taken by him and others in his life. Actions can better be discussed than feelings. Discussion of feelings will take place later.

Initiation

The next step in counseling after engagement is initiation or change or movement. Some people call this the "work phase." No matter what the term, this is where the counselor's focus, direction, and goal setting begin to try to influence the client to change his thoughts, feelings, and/or behaviors.

For most counselors goal-setting takes place at this point and sometimes in the first session. Goal-setting is very important not only because it gives a baseline upon which to evaluate the progress of the client in the change process but also it makes the counseling process more concrete. Men need to see that counseling is about making changes in their lives. I suggest that both long-term and short-term goals are established. I also believe that the client should be informed that changes don't usually happen immediately and that his life is likely to get worse before it gets better. I try to warn clients who have unrealistic expectations of counseling and of themselves.

A suggestion about goal-setting is to have the client be actively involved in setting the goals. It will make him invested in the process. You can alter and shape the goals with the client into behavioral and measurable terms.

One warning about goal-setting is to avoid letting clients set goals that are directed towards making other people act differently. We can try to make others like us, respect us, marry us or promote us, but there's no guarantee. We can help clients to become more likeable, worthy of respect, worthy of marrying, or more worthy of promotion, and that's all. The rest is up to chance.

At the beginning of the initiation stage, I also do an evaluation, usually very informally, of the client's level of awareness of his symptoms, his feelings, and of the causes of his behaviors. I ask about his weight gain or loss, sleeping patterns, headaches, chronic pains, prescription medications taken regularly, alcohol and/or drug use, changes in social patterns, and the reports of others about him. I note if the client sees a connection between these symptoms and the concern that brought him in to see me. Some clients do, others do not. I will try to make the connections as we go forward.

I try to see if the client is aware of feelings. This is a difficult process because they usually respond with their thoughts not feelings. I don't challenge them at this early stage about a difficulty in identifying their feelings. I usually label clients' described feelings as "lousy", as in "that must have made you feel lousy." With some clients I refer to a hypothetical man by saying, "Lots of men would have been pretty angry in that situation." I'm trying to normalize having feelings.

Finally, I try to determine clients' awareness of any causes of their distress. I don't want them to blame other people for their misfortune, but more to identify the events and relationships that have shaped their expectations of themselves and others, and coping styles.

To gain a sense of these three awarenesses, I often ask men to bring in parts of their lives that will allow me to gain access to their more guarded thoughts and feelings. I have asked men to bring in family photo albums dating back to their childhood. I've asked for a family history, high school and college yearbooks, scrapbooks and collections they have established. The plan is to use personal objects to prompt clients to reveal aspects of themselves. I ask questions such as, "What were you like back then?" "What are you like now?" and "What makes you happy?"

Sometimes to get a better idea of how men behave, I role-play. I will be the boss, spouse, child or whoever is a problem person for the client, and the client will play himself using his typical behavior. The client will set the scene and tell me how to behave. We will do a brief role play, no more than 3 to 5 minutes, and then I'll ask him if his role play was similar to how he acts in the outside world. I will have a better idea of how he acts and so will he. This is a powerful tool not just for my data gathering, but also for initiating change on the client's part. We can begin to examine his thoughts and feelings about his behavior and his assessment about the appropriateness and effectiveness of his behavior. We can then generate options and practice them.

Some men relate well to readings, movies or on-line resources. I give them suggestion of books that seem to fit them. I've recommended *I Remember* by Dan Rather that details the struggle of a young boy and a distant father. Another book about fathers and sons is *Sons on Father: A book of men's writings* by Ralph Keyes. I avoid the autobiographies of sports figures, statesmen, or others whose lives seem to be too glamorous and unrealistic.

Some can benefit from movies or television programs that portray men in realistic struggles, such as with difficult fathers in *The Great Santini*. I dislike the "buddy" films, which I believe are unrealistic and superficial. I also dislike the heroic films that only serve to perpetuate the male myth that is destructive to ordinary men of today. Some websites that can be useful for men include menstuff.org, themenscenter.com, and menweb.org.

Books that are helpful for counselors include *Handbook of Counseling and Psychotherapy with Men* edited by Scher, Stevens, Good, and Eichenfield, *The New Handbook of Counseling and Psychotherapy with Men* edited by Brooks and Good, *Men in Groups* by Andronico, *A New Psychology of Men* edited by Levant and Pollack, and *Masculinity Reconstructed: Changing the Rules of Manhood-at Work, in Relationships, and in Family Life* by Levant and Kopecky. Counselors also might wish to investigate Division 51 of the American Psychological Association, the Society for the Psychological Study of Men and Masculinity.

For Family and Friends

With men in your life, I suggest that you never tell them, "What you should do is...." Don't make suggestions, instead extend invitations to join you. I believe that the most effective approach is not prescriptive. Telling men what you think they should do for themselves or what you believe is good for them will likely feel demeaning or patronizing to them, no matter how well the message is delivered. This approach is just too direct and threatening. In place of advice-giving, extend an offer for them to do something with you. It will be asking them to do a favor for you. It's a request for them to accompany you in an activity that you would like to do.

With this strategy in mind, suggest that you do things that break the existing routine of daily events. We all enjoy routines because they give us the peace and security of familiarity and reliability. That's fine, but variety gives us new perspectives and challenges. Some men need the challenges in order to learn new behaviors that will gain them power and intimacy. Going to new places gives men the opportunities to try out new behaviors. Asking a man to let you join him on his trip to the hardware store doesn't sound like much, but how many people have done it? Suggest to a man that instead of going alone to the mall, he goes with you.

Breaking routines doesn't mean breaking them forever, just alter the routine temporarily. Finding new places such as restaurants, vacation spots and weekend day-trips are all good ideas.

Adding a new activity such as biking, outdoor cooking, or yoga might be interesting. Starting a hobby never seems to work well as men often start these activities as solo projects and quickly drop them. They would be more likely to continue, I believe, if done with someone else. The idea is not to have men do more activities alone. They're alone enough.

New people are often a good idea. Meeting new people can be difficult but not impossible. Everyone probably has some co-workers who might be enjoyable and interesting to get to know outside of the work setting. Neighbors also can be a source of people to get to know better. People from the past are also good, but are a bigger risk to contact. We all have people around us with whom we've lost touch but would welcome a phone call and an invitation to get together. There's no guarantee that a friendship might be rekindled, but the idea is to practice new social skills and break the routine.

Incidentally, socializing with new people one-on-one or in a group is an important consideration. Some men prefer smaller numbers of people; e.g., another person at lunch. Others prefer couple-to-couple activity. Still others feel better in crowds so a small party is the best idea. It all depends on the comfort level of the person. I think a crowd is easiest for many men as the number of people and the brevity and superficiality of many conversations there minimize the level of intimacy. A one-to-one activity has, perhaps, the most chance for openness and intimacy.

In order to move ahead sometimes we have to look at the past. An easy way to do this is to help men look at significant periods in their past, such as high school, college, or military service. Asking men to recall their past experience during these time periods may help them gain perspectives on themselves. Ask them to look at their high school or college yearbook. Go with them to attend a reunion. Go with them to the old hometown, campus, or military base separate from a reunion. Ask them what they were like back then, and what they're like now. As we are in the day of electronic communication, see if there is a blog centered on the old cohort of colleagues. Suggest they join a local alumni group. Reconnecting with specific former friends is easy due to Internet searches and email.

In therapy I sometimes encourage men to keep a journal, which they will review and discuss with me, but I don't suggest that family and friends make this suggestion. I don't want men to do any more solitary activities. Instead, I suggest that family and friends ask the man in their lives to write an autobiography or story about a specific time period or event in their lives if a complete autobiography seems to be too large a task. In this way men can see that it's a task with an acceptable purpose, because men write books all the time. They don't have to ever submit it for publication. It's only for their personal use and a way of communicating to their family and friends about themselves. I remember one man sharing with me his written story about his relationship with his recently deceased dog. It was a very poignant and revealing story and showed a side of him not seen, I believe, by many other people.

Another way to review the past is to examine photograph albums, home movies, scrapbooks, and other memorabilia. Ask men about what they were doing first, and then what they were like at the time the record was made. Ask them if they keep memorabilia in their office or home. I know one man (in his sixties) who keeps his high school baseball glove in the study in his home.

In a different vein, involve men in non-competitive physical events. Go with them on a bike ride, to work out at a health club, or attend a yoga class. I know that men would prefer tennis, racket ball, or bowling, where one wins and loses or at least keeps score, but I want them to break the routine. The goal of non-competitive physical activity is gaining awareness, in addition to fitness. Going for a brief walk is a good place to start.

I think that volunteering is a good place to meet people and to gain a sense of power and intimacy. Helping others makes men feel worthwhile and allows for intimacy among fellow volunteers. Finding the right activity is the key. Churches, community groups, homeowners, political parties, and special interest groups all offer a range of opportunities from special events, such as fundraisers to ongoing work. I know one man is a reader for a group that records books for blind and dyslectic people. I believe there is something for everyone.

Looking toward the end of life, I suggest that men get help to make a will. Almost half the people in our country die without making a will, which can cause stress and financial complications for the surviving family members. My purpose in suggesting that you engage the man in your life in making a will is not only to make the legal exchange of property easier but also to help the man think about his current life. Books on making wills are in every bookstore. Buy a book, read the material and then have a meeting during which you discuss the plan. In most books one is advised to make an inventory of property, assets and debts. Ask him about the current state of his life and how he feels about it. It has a lot to do with power. How a man feels about his accumulated possessions can be very revealing. The goal is not to have the man work harder to accumulate more assets but to have him see that his time is limited and a rebalancing of power and intimacy may need to be done.

Finally, for a few men, self-help books might be worthwhile. Few men read them. Most are written for women who want to change the man or men in their lives. I suggest that you find a book that seems to be non-threatening and read it yourself first. Then ask the man in your life to read sections that you've highlighted or noted. Make these sections no more than a few pages long, not entire chapters. Tell him you would like his opinion on the section and need his help in understanding what the author means or if the author is correct about his or her point. This lets the man be the helper and interpreter not the recipient of help. Then a discussion can be held where you may be able to assist your man to think about himself with respect to the reading material.

Some people might think that I'm advocating manipulation or that I'm demeaning the intelligence of men. I'm not. I'm suggesting an indirect approach rather than a direct one. The indirect approach has the potential of engaging men more effectively than direct approaches, because defenses are less likely to be immediately aroused. Keeping psychological defenses low is an acceptable way of helping others. You're not doing something that takes unfair advantage of men. You're trying to do something that will benefit their lives.

References

Andronico, M. (Ed.). (1996). *Men in groups: Insights interventions, and psychoeducational work*. Washington, DC: American Psychological Association.

Bly, J. (1990). *Iron John*. Reading, MA: Addison-Wesley.

Brooks, G. & Good, G. (Eds.). (2001). *The new handbook of psychotherapy and counseling with men*. New York: John Wiley & Sons.

Buffett, J. (1998). *A pirate looks at fifty*. New York: Fawcett Books.

Burns, D. (1980). *Feeling good: The new mood therapy*. New York: Avon Books.

Clatterbaugh, K. (1990). *Contemporary perspectives on masculinity: Men, women, politics in modern society*. Boulder, CO: Westview Press.

Diamond, J. (1997). *Male menopause*. New York: Sourcebooks Trade.

Farrell, W. (1986). *Why men are the way they are*. New York: Penguin.

Goldberg, H. (1976). *The hazards of being male*. New York: Nash.

Heifner, C. (1997). The male experience of depression. *Perspectives in Psychiatric Care, 33*, 10-18.

Hite, S. (1987). *Women and love*. New York: Knopf.

Keen, S. (1991). *Fire in the belly: On being a man*. New York: Bantam Books.

Kimmel, M. (1997). *Manhood in America*. New York: Free Press.

Kiley, D. (1983). *The Peter Pan syndrome*. New York: Dodd, Mead.

Lasn, K. (1999). *Culture jam*. New York: Perennial

Levant, R.F. (1996). The new psychology of men. *Professional Psychology: Research and Practice, 27*, 259-265.

Levant, R.F. & Kopecky, G. (1994). *Masculinity reconstructed: Changing the rules of manhood at work, in relationships, and in family life.* New York: Dutton.

Levant, R.F. & Pollack, W.S. (Eds.). (1995). *A new psychology of men.* New York: Basic Books.

Levinson, D. (1978). *The seasons of a man's life.* New York: Knopf.

Mahalik, J. R. (1999). Incorporating a gender role strain perspective in assessing and treating men's cognitive distortions. *Professional Psychology: Research and Practice, 30*, 333-34

Pittman, F. (1993). *Man enough: Fathers, sons, and the search for masculinity.* New York: Putnam.

Peck, M. S. (1978). *The road less traveled: A new psychology of love, traditional values, and spritual growth.* New York: Touchstone Books.

Pleck, J.H. (1981). *The myth of masculinity.* Cambridge: MIT Press.

Pleck, J.H. (1995). The gender role strain paradigm. An update. In R.F. Levant & W. S. Pollack (Eds.) *A new psychology of men.* (pp. 11-32). New York: Basic Books.

Pollack, W.S. (1995). No man is an island. In R.F. Levant & W. S. Pollack (Eds.) *A new psychology of men.* (pp. 33-67). New York: Basic Books.

Sheehy, G. (1999). *Understanding men's passages.* New York: Ballantine.

Spence, G. (1995). *How to argue and win every time.* New York: St. Martin's Press.

Tiger, L. (1999). *The decline of males.* New York: St. Martin's.

Vaillant, G.E. (1995). *The wisdom of ego: Sources of resilience in adult life.* New York: Balknap.

Waehler, C. A. (1996). *Bachelors: The psychology of men who haven't married.* Westport, CT: Praeger.

Index

activities, dropped, 102
affairs, 152–153
age progression, 127–132
age thirty, 49–52
age thirty, after, 52–54
aggressiveness, 3–4
agreeable terminology, 167
alcohol, 26
alexithymia, 3
"American Dream," 12, 17
Andronico, M., 173
anger, expressing, 24
anger management, 25
anticipatory anxiety, 157, 158
anxiety, 13–15
   anticipatory, 157
   awareness of, 158
   debilitating, 158
   living with, 158–160
approach, indirect, 176–177
assessment techniques,
attractiveness, 50
   in midlife, 134–135
attribution bias theory, 30
authority figure or pal, 169
autobiographies, 172
avoidance, 107
avoidance of confrontation, 13–15
awareness, 171–172
   of anxiety, 158
   of feelings and causes, 28
   of symptoms, 27–28

Bachelors: The psychology of men who haven't married, 71

balancing power and intimacy, 48
battery analogy, 91, 111–112
behavior, learned, 3
best friend, 38–39
blame in divorce, 117
blending families, 126
Bly, J., 3
boredom
   beating, 153–154
   and marital break-up, 151–153
Brooks and Good, 173
"buddy" films, 172
Buffett, Jimmy, 159
burnout in marriage, 111–113
Burns, David, 159

career
   autonomy in, 90
   change, 56–57
   concerns in midlife, 132–133
   dissatisfaction, 55–56
   home/office, 64–65
   insecurity, 54–55
   reality, 54–57
   vs. family, 66–67
causes, awareness of, 171–172
change, fear of, 131–132
change or consolidation, 128–129
childcare
   avoiding, 80
   sharing, 79
child custody, 113–116
childish/child-like, 107

children, 64, 78–80
    activities of, 146–148
    and divorce, 120–121
    hers/his/theirs, 125–126
    and never-married man, 139–140
children, adult, 136–137
child, second, 65–66
cog-in-the-wheel, 67
commitment, 155–156
community service and never-married man, 141
compensating activities, 96–97
competence
    diminished, 74–75
    need for, 5
competition, 143–144, 161
competition, avoiding, 18
confidentiality, 166
conflict
    between power/intimacy, 4–5
    coping with, 13–14
confrontation, avoidance of, 13–15
consolidation or change, 128–129
consolidation pattern, 127–128
contract, marital, 112–113
cooperation, 161
co-parenting, 115–116
coping with anxiety, 159
counselors
    gender of, 165–166
    working with men, 165–173
couple, half of, 39–41
couples in midlife, 145–146
credentials, professional, 167
crises, men's, 4
cues, 24–25
Culture Jam, 35
custody,
    child, 113–116
    double binds of, 114–115

dating during separation, 118–119, 121–122
defense mechanisms, 9

denial, 107
depression
    acute or chronic?, 30
    sub-clinical, 23–24
    symptoms of, 25–26
    underdiagnosed, 24
depression and rage, 10, 23–27
de-sexualization of friendships, 68–69
Diamond, J., 4
diminished competence, 74–75
discipline of children, 78–79
disclosure, too much, 54
"Disneyland" parent, 115
divorce, 82–84, 97, 111
    blame in, 117
    as defeat, 83
    and fatherhood, 83–84
    and money, 121
    and social scene, 137–138
    telling children about, 120–121
dominance, level of, 124
double binds of custody, 114–115
drugs, 26
dysfunction, sexual, 77–78
dysthymia, 24

effort as yardstick, 159
emotional burnout, 112
emotional intimacy, 9
emotions, hiding, 15–16
empty nest, 136–137
encounter, initial, 165
energy, unlimited, 91–92
engagement, 165–170
enough for everyone, 162
escape, 62, 86, 97
    planned/unplanned, 104–105
expectations, unrealistic, 171

failure, fear of, 3–4, 73, 106–107
families, blending, 126
family
    and counseling, 173–177
    and divorce, 120–121

as respite, 90–91
fantasy, parental, 11–12
Farrell, W., 3
father
    divorced, 83–84
    and stepchildren, 125–126
fatherhood, 64
    responsibility of, 81–82
fathers and sons, 10, 11–13, 172
fathers as examples, 156, 29
fear of change, 131–132
feedback, 144, 159
Feeling Good, 159
feelings
    awareness of, 171
    denial of, 97–98
    hiding, 4
feeling vs thinking, 129
financial insecurity, 94–95
financial security, 89
Finding our Fathers, 13, 156
Fire in the Belly, 3
forces men face, 160–162
forties crisis, avoiding, 52–53
forty, not ready for, 130–131
friendships, 89–90
    and men, 145–146
    and never-married man, 140
    with women, 68–69
friendships, continuing old, 68

Galper, Miriam, 116
gathering information, 170
goal-setting, 170–171
goals of book, vii
Goldberg, H, 3
The Great Santini, 172
group activities, 102
group counseling, 135

habits, good and bad, 168
Handbook of Counseling and Psychotherapy with Men, 173
The Hazards of Being Male, 3
Heifner, C., 24

help one person, 162
hiding emotions, 15–16
HIPAA regulations, 166
homework, 170
How to Argue and Win Every Time, 160

identity development, male, 2
important/scary, 163
independence, 72–74
information gathering, 170
initiation, 170–173
insecurity, career, 54–55
insecurity, sexual, 42–44
insurance matters, privacy in, 166
integration of power and intimacy, 18–23, 47–48
intimacy, 8–9, 155
intimacy
    avoiding, 15–18
    defined, 8
    levels of, 47
    recognizing the need for, 22–23
intimacy and power
    balancing, 18–23, 48
invulnerability, shell of, 20
I Only Say This Because I Love You, 156
I Remember, 172
Iron John, 3
irresponsibility, appropriate, 107–108
isolation, 72–73

jargon, 167
Jekyll and Hyde, 17
Joint Custody and Co-Parenting, 116
journal, keeping a, 175
journey theme, 162

Keen, S., 3
Keyes, Ralph, 172
Kimmel, M., 3

Lally, Tara, ix
language, non-clinical, 167
Lasn, Kalle, 35
learned behavior, 24
leisure activities, 112–113
   and never-married man, 141
Levant & Kopecky, 173
Levant & Pollack, 5, 173
Levinson, D., 4
life plan, 130–131
   adjustments to, 87–94
   at thirty, 85–87
life stages, viii
life themes, 15–18, 162–163
loneliness, 72
   after divorce, 122–123
   in midlife, 137–138
love, 155–156

machine, man as, 97–99
machismo/macho, 4, 10
Mahalik, J. R., 3
male identity development, 2
male ideology, 5–6
Man Enough, 3
Manhood in America, 3
marital break-up
   and boredom, 151–153
   reasons for, 148–154
marital relationships, 46–47
marriage
   adjustment after, 74
   burnout, 111–113
   maintenance, 143–148
   readiness for, 71–72
   and status, 46
   at thirty, 61–64
Masculinity Reconstructed, 173
maturity, accepting, 50–51
memorabilia, 175
Men in Groups, 173
middle adulthood
   activities dropped, 102
   challenges of, 101
   changes during, 85–86
   crossroads, 58
   tiredness in, 111
mid-life
   crisis, 4, 56, 94, 131
   and never-married man, 138–140
   problems, 132–137
midpoint,
   chronological, 129
moment, in the, 162
money, 74–75
   and divorce, 121
   and second marriage, 125
mothers, myth of, 80–81
mother, working, 64–65
motorcycle, 63
moving out during separation, 121

Nance, Don, ix
needs, fundamental, 5
never-married man
   and children, 139–140
   guidelines for, 140–141
   in midlife, 138–140
The New Handbook of Counseling and Psychotherapy with Men, 173
A New Psychology of Men, 173

office privacy, 166
old/young, 49, 129–130
orientation, 167–169
Osherson, Samuel, 12–13, 13, 156

pack member, 38
pal or authority figure, 169
parent
   "Disneyland," 115
   "throw-away," 114–115
parties, 154
passion, 155–156
Peck, M. Scott, 159
peers at work, 143–145
phone contact privacy, 166
physical ability, fear of losing, 50

physical activities, 175
physical ailments and marital break-up, 149
physical signs in midlife, 133–134
A Pirate Looks at Fifty, 159
Pittman, F. S., 3
planfulness, 102
power, 4–8
  definition of, 5
  denying need for, 17–18
  expectations of, 11–12
  maintaining, 9
  measurements of, 5
  misuse of, 98
  and security, 95–96
  seeking, 16–17
  validation of, 7
  and work, 33
power and intimacy
  balancing, 18–23, 48
  choice between, 9–10, 20–21
  conflict between, 4–5
  search for, 2
priorities, for men/women, 155
privacy in counseling, 166
progression, age, 127–132
purposes of book, 1–2

rage and depression, 10
Rather, Dan, 172
readiness for marriage, 71–72
recalling the past, 174–175
re-charging, necessary, 91
reconciliation, 116, 120
recreation patterns, 90
re-entry phase after separation, 119
referrals, 169–170
reflection on life, 52–53
relationships
  avoiding, 60–61
  coworkers, 34–36
  marital, 46–47
  sexual, 41–46
  social, 36–38
  at thirty, 53–54

relaxation, 113
relocation, job, 103
remarriage, 122–126
resentment, 106–107
responsibility, 29–30, 57
  pressure of, 61–64
  price of, 106–107
right thing, do the, 162
right woman, in second marriage, 123–124
The Road Less Traveled, 159
Roberts-Wilbur, Janice, 114
role playing, 172
routine and never-married man, 140–141
routines, breaking, 173–174
rut, escaping from, 104

safest path, 96
same team, 162
satisfaction
  with choices made, 92–93
scary/important, 163
Scher, Stevens, Good & Eichenfield, 173
searching for mate, 58–60
second marriage
  and money, 125
  right woman in, 123–124
self-disclosure by client, 169
self-help books, 176
self-medication, 26
self-sacrifice of needs, 62–64
separation, 116–117
  dating during, 118–119, 121–122
  duration of, 117–120
  and moving out, 121
  sex during, 121–122
"settling" for less, 86–87
sex, 75–78
  during separation, 121–122
sexual
  decline and marital break-up, 150–151

dysfunction, 77–78
insecurity, 42–44
performance in midlife, 135–136
relationships, 41–46
shared activities, 154
"shutdown," 107
social
  life, 94
  patterns, 38–41
  pressure, 50–51
  reality, 58
  relationships, 36–38
  scene, 101–103
  scene in midlife, 137–141
socializing, 174
societal roles for men, 3
societal standards
  for men, 2, 6–8, 10
Society for the Psychological Study of Men and Masculinity (APA), 173
sons and fathers, 10, 11–13, 156, 172
Sons on Father, 172
Spence, Gerry, 160
spontaneity, 102
sports, group, 102
sports metaphor, 157
"stage fright," 157
"start over"
  and divorce, 111
  at midlife, 138
status and marriage, 46
status, social pressure for, 50–51
stepping back, 99
  stereotype, male, 1
  symptoms, awareness of, 171

Tannen, Deborah, 156
techniques, assessment, 2
television, turn off, 154
terminology, agreeable, 167
themes, life, 162–163
thinking vs feeling, 129

"throw-away" parent, 114–115
time limit, set, 168
tiredness in middle adulthood, 111
touching, 154
"tough guy," 3
traditions, family, 12–13
"training," 89, 90
transition at thirty, 52–54, 68
trial-and-error, 34, 35, 42, 57
triggers, 24–25

unfulfilled fantasy, 11–12

Vaillant, G.E., 4
Viagra, 136
volunteering, 175–176
vulnerability, 73

Waehler, Charles, 71
Why Men are the Way they Are, 3
widowed and the social scene, 137–138
wife
  and lifestyle changes, 108–10
  working, 64–65
  young, 81–82
will, making a, 176
"wimp," 3, 109–110
Winheld, Amy, ix
work
  and early adulthood, 33
  and home separation, 17
  and marital break-up, 14
  and peers, 143–145
  and relationships, 60–61
work challenges, 94–95
working together, 167
"work phase," 170
Wormser, Ron, ix

young/old, 49, 129–130

About the Author

Dr. Gordon Hart is a licensed psychologist who has worked with clients for over 30 years in private practice. Many of his clients have been men who have been seen in either individual counseling or as a member of a couple. He has consulted with organizations and schools on issues of conflict management. He is also a full professor in the Counseling Psychology Program at Temple University and is director of the doctoral program. He teaches master's and doctoral level courses and does research. He has supervised over 200 graduate students in their clinical work and has directed the dissertation research of 70 doctoral students. He, his wife and their dog live in suburban Philadelphia.

HQ1090 .H37 2006

Hart, Gordon M

Power and intimacy in men's
development JUN 1 6 2006